CONFLICT & COMPROMISE IN HISTORY

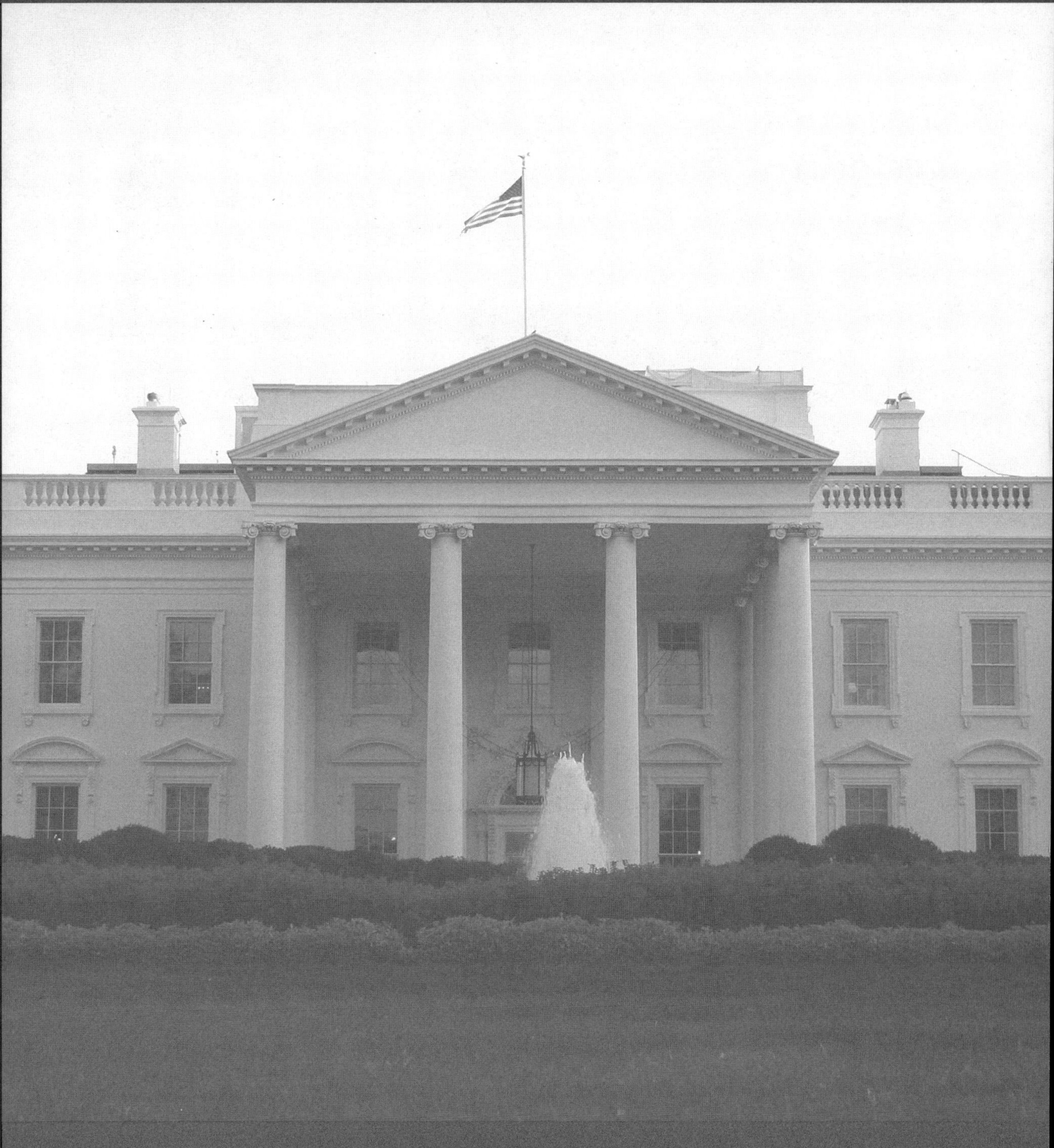

THE PRESIDENCY
Resource Book

NHD NATIONAL HISTORY DAY

ABC-CLIO Schools

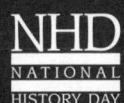

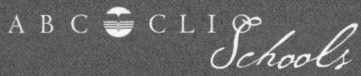

ABC-CLIO

PROJECT EDITOR
Holly Leck, *Manager, Resource Book Development*

EDITORIAL
Lynn Jurgensen, *Editorial Manager*
David Tipton, *Editorial Manager*
Kirk Werner, *Manager, Editorial Operations, Content Archiving, and Print Design*
Holly Heinzer, *Manager, Editorial Development*
Jennifer Hutchinson, *Writer/Editor*
Marian Perales, *Writer/Editor*
Gregory Wolf, *Writer/Editor*
Adena Boghos, *Editorial Assistant*
Jane Messah, *Editorial Assistant*
Lauren Thomas, *Editorial Assistant*

MEDIA ACQUISITIONS
Katherine Jackson, *Media Production Coordinator*
Caroline Price, *Manager, Media Resources*

PRODUCTION
Don Schmidt, *Manager, Books Production*
Anna A. Moore, *Production Editor*
Vicki Moran, *Senior Production Editor*
Paula Gerard, *File Management Coordinator*

National History Day, Inc.

Ann Claunch, *Director of Curriculum*

DESIGN
The Winter Group

COPYRIGHT © 2007 BY ABC-CLIO, INC.
All rights reserved. Permission is granted to reproduce lesson material for classroom use only.

Library of Congress Cataloging-in-Publication Data
Conflict & compromise in history : the Presidency : resource book / ABC-CLIO.
　　p. cm.
　Includes bibliographical references.
　ISBN 978-1-59884-116-9 (workbook : alk. paper) 1. Presidents--United States. 2. Presidents--United States--History. 3. United States--Politics and government. I. ABC-Clio Information Services. II. Title: Conflict and compromise in history. III. Title: Presidency.
　JK516.C56 2007
　352.230973--dc22　　　　　　　　　　　　　　　2007005993

COVER PHOTO: Front view of the White House and gardens in Washington, D.C. (iStockPhoto.com)

Contents

iv About the Development Team
vi Foreword
viii Using This Resource Book
xi Preface

1 INTRODUCTION
Resolving International Crises

11 THROUGHOUT HISTORY
From 1787 to Today

25 DEFINING MOMENT I
President Wilson and the League of Nations
   28 Classroom Activities
   46 Primary and Secondary Sources
   64 Background Material

75 DEFINING MOMENT II
Roosevelt at the Yalta Conference
   78 Classroom Activities
   96 Primary and Secondary Sources
   121 Background Material

134 ADDITIONAL RESOURCES
   135 Integration into National History Day
   137 Using ABC-CLIO Websites for Researching the Presidency
   138 Additional Presidency Topic Ideas

About the Development Team

SETH MASKET
UNIVERSITY OF DENVER

Seth Masket received his Ph.D. in political science from the University of California, Los Angeles. He also holds an M.A. in political science from George Washington University and a B.A. in political science from the University of California at Berkeley. Seth is an assistant professor at the University of Denver who specializes in American politics, particularly political parties and campaigns at the local, state, and national levels. Prior to his academic career, Seth was a senior writer in the White House Office of Correspondence under President Clinton. He also worked as a research assistant at the Woodrow Wilson International Center in Washington, D.C.

CHRIS MULLIN
SANTA YNEZ VALLEY UNION HIGH SCHOOL

Chris Mullin graduated from the University of California at Berkeley with a degree in classical Greek and Latin and received his master's degree in education from the University of California at Santa Barbara. Chris teaches Latin, Advanced Placement European history, and Advanced Placement United States history in the beautiful Santa Ynez Valley, California, at Santa Ynez Valley Union High School. Chris has been a fellow of the Teachers Network Leadership Institute and a facilitator for the California History-Social Science Project; he has developed numerous history-related classroom activities that he has presented at state and national conferences. In 2003, Chris was named California Teacher of the Year for his passionate and innovative approaches to teaching history. Chris is dedicated to finding innovative ways to introduce primary source materials into the day-to-day teaching of history. He believes in challenging students and encouraging them to see history not as a series of verifiable facts but as a compendium of open-ended questions. In lectures, he makes a point of revealing his own reflective process to help students hone their own critical thinking skills.

THE PRESIDENCY

BRETT PIERSMA
SANTA YNEZ VALLEY UNION HIGH SCHOOL

Brett Piersma received his B.A. in history and his master's degree in education and teaching credential at the University of California at Santa Barbara. He teaches Advanced Placement European history, Advanced Placement American government, and college preparatory world cultures at Santa Ynez Valley Union High School in Santa Ynez, California. He has facilitated the California History-Social Sciences Project at UCSB and is a MetLife Fellow for the Teachers Network Leadership Institute. Brett has also co-written several award-winning classroom activities. His many passions in teaching include designing primary source–based lesson plans, increasing teacher voice and leadership in schools, increasing student access to rigorous curricula, and perfecting the use of technology in the classroom. Among his innovative techniques are dress-up nights for Advanced Placement European history students that recreate an Enlightenment-era *salon,* complete with period music and debates on the works of Voltaire and Rousseau.

Foreword

The *Conflict & Compromise in History* series explores three institutions that represent American freedom: the presidency, citizen soldiers, and the women's rights movement. Although the Declaration of Independence and the Constitution set the ideals for our nation, the real meaning for the word *freedom* has come through conflicting interpretations of the ideology. These conflicts can be traced through history by a series of recursive questions asked of the government. The citizen soldier has been trapped in a tug-of-war since the American Revolution with an ongoing debate on the defense of the United States in times of crisis: *Who should defend America—a professional army or a volunteer force?* Through the early women's movement the question voiced created a firestorm of response, and the conflict continues today, as women fight more subtle inequalities: *When will women have equal rights?* The Office of the President faces questions of response to national and international conflicts: *When do we respond to conflict and when do we compromise?*

These questions continue to be debated and answered by the historical time and place in which they are confronted. In the *Conflict & Compromise in History* series the institutions of the presidency, citizen soldiers, and the women's right movement will be examined through the decision-making processes. We will discuss when the responses have come through conflict or through compromise, or when a response has contained a combination of both.

At their center, these resource books are devoted to providing students with the raw materials to evaluate each issue for themselves. In each book, students will find a wide array of primary materials: laws, poems, quotations, cartoons, speeches, editorials, and images. To help students interpret these historical documents and give them a solid grounding in the topic, secondary essays, glossaries, and background material are provided as well. This material also represents a great variety of sources, drawn from experts in diverse fields including education, political science, history, and literature.

Together, these primary and secondary sources form the building blocks for sets of classroom activities. These activities are designed to encourage students to analyze primary documents and to use their conclusions to evaluate the ways that the presidency, citizen soldiers, and the women's right movement have been handled throughout past centuries. Students are asked to debate, to role play, and to write creatively about the historical materials. At the conclusion of the activity, the students are asked to judge the actions of the parties involved and to unravel the complexities within each issue.

Opening each resource book, you will find a series of essays designed to introduce students to each topic. The first essay is a broad issue overview. The second essay is more specific and chronological. Next, the books present two "Defining Moments"—landmark historical events that illustrate the nature of debate on each topic. Each Defining Moment section begins with detailed background information. Then you will find the classroom activities, with instructions and a list of materials needed to complete them. These materials, primary sources and reference pieces, follow each classroom activity section. The activities are broken down into parts, each one designed to challenge the students' assumptions and lead them to different conclusions. The last portion of the activity asks the students to assess both the Defining Moment and the larger issue.

In partnering to compile the *Conflict & Compromise in History* series of resource books, ABC-CLIO and National History Day, Inc. continue their commitment to challenging students with historical material that both celebrates and complicates our concept of the national heritage. By combining quality research with active learning, we hope to bring the excitement of lively history and participatory civics to your classroom.

BECKY SNYDER
PRESIDENT, SCHOOLS PUBLISHER
ABC-CLIO

CATHY GORN
EXECUTIVE DIRECTOR
National History Day

Using This Resource Book

The *Conflict & Compromise in History* resource books are designed to provide teachers with all the materials to create interactive lessons centered on a single important topic of American history. In each lesson, students are asked to analyze primary historical documents and draw conclusions about the topic. You will find two sets of suggested classroom activities in each book. For each activity, we have provided background essays, source documents, and reference pieces.

THE MATERIALS ARE ORGANIZED AS FOLLOWS:

1. INTRODUCTION
The essay in this section is a broad overview of the resource book's topic. You may use it to create a general lesson or lecture on the issue at hand, or to prepare students for the historical analysis portions.

2. THROUGHOUT HISTORY
The material provided here is geared to a specific subtopic within the broader issue—for example, the impact of civil rights initiatives on the women's movement, or foreign policy approaches of various presidents. This material may be used to create a preparatory lecture for the resource book's interactive portions or copied and handed out for students to read.

3. DEFINING MOMENTS I AND II
Each resource book features two "defining moments," spotlights on significant events in history that illustrate key issues related to the overall theme of the book. Each defining moment contains an introduction, a series of classroom activities, primary and secondary sources, and background material. Following is a description of each of these four sections.

a. Introduction
The Defining Moment section begins with a short historical background essay that provides context for the classroom activities. Again, this piece may be used to organize a short presentation or given to students to read before they begin the activities.

b. Classroom Activities

Each Defining Moment includes a series of Classroom Activities. The Activity is broken down into lessons, and the materials required for each lesson are noted. When the lesson calls for Activity Sheets, these are located with the Activity description. In some cases, portions of the Activity may stand alone, but they are designed to be cumulative. The last part draws on the lessons of the earlier parts, making it the most comprehensive. Some lessons are designed to take up a full class period, some are shorter, and some require homework assignments. The teacher should determine what is appropriate for his or her class based upon allotted time and teaching goals.

c. Primary and Secondary Sources

The historical documents, images, cartoons, and other materials called for in the Classroom Activities are in this section; each piece is designed to be reproduced for the students. In most cases, the teacher should create handouts of these materials; when the sources are used to stimulate class discussions, he or she can make overheads.

d. Background Material

After the Primary Sources are reference sources such as glossary words, biographies, information on important laws, and descriptions of relevant events. The teacher may wish to make handouts or overheads of this material or write some of the information on the board to help students with unfamiliar vocabulary or concepts.

4. ADDITIONAL RESOURCES

The end of the book highlights three additional ways students can further their research of the general topic. The Integration into National History Day overview presents ideas for student projects and demonstrates how the topics in the resource book can support them. Next is Using the ABC-CLIO Websites for Researching, a brief description of the ways the ABC-CLIO websites can assist students in narrowing their topics, identifying relevant sources, and analyzing what they find. Finally, a section entitled Additional Topic Ideas lists a number of topics related to the resource book titles that students might be interested in studying.

We hope you find this format user-friendly and that you are able to adapt it easily to fit your students' needs.

Preface

For young adults, it is simply not enough to read texts about vital issues at the heart of American citizenship. Like the generations before them, our students are going to grapple with these topics in their lifetimes. They need to prepare by turning a critical eye on the histories of the presidency, citizen soldiers, and the women's movement. Their understanding of the past will help them to make sense of the present and to make informed decisions in the future. Teaching students to examine these issues as they relate to the theme of *Conflict & Compromise in History* will provide a framework with which students can push past the antiquated view of history as mere facts and dates and drill down into historical content to develop perspective and understanding.

Students sometimes learn history fast and without meaning. The discipline is vast, and the current educational climate emphasizes coverage of content over depth. Class design is often determined by time periods and approached chronologically. But without a guiding framework, students are abandoned to isolated pieces of historical information. A theme redefines how history is learned. Instead of concentrating on the whole century or a broad topic, students are invited to stop and analyze a smaller event, a part of the story, and place it in the context of the whole. Teaching with a theme ensures that students are not overwhelmed with the sheer vastness of the field but instead are invited to look deeply into a manageable portion of history.

Conflict & Compromise in History provides students with a lens through which to read history, an organizational structure that helps them to place information in the correct context, and finally, the ability to see connections over time. We invite your students to extend their study of the presidency, citizen soldiers, and the women's rights movement by engaging in active research and presentation.

(Hulton-Deutsch Collection/Corbis)

INTRODUCTION

Resolving International Crises

INTRODUCTION

Resolving International Crises

AUTHOR

Seth Masket
University of Denver

This resource book addresses the question of how U.S. presidents have dealt with diplomacy in foreign affairs during conflicts and crises. Over the course of U.S. history, presidents have tended to rely increasingly on the art of compromise in foreign diplomacy. While foreign negotiations were usually veiled in secrecy before the twentieth century, attempts were eventually made to achieve more transparency in these proceedings. For example, despite the failure of the League of Nations, open negotiations were generally achieved after the formation of the United Nations—a negotiating world body developed to address conflicts without resorting to immediate aggression. Later, foreign diplomacy took place within the arena of summit conferences like those that have been held at Camp David, Reykjavik, and Moscow.

While they have undergone many permutations over the past two centuries, the foundations of power in foreign policy were established in the U.S. Constitution. The president is our nation's lead diplomat, empowered by the Constitution to "receive ambassadors and other public ministers." It is the president, or those he directly appoints, who negotiates treaties with other nations. Additionally, the Constitution provides the president with considerable authority as the commander in chief of the U.S. armed forces. The preeminent role of the United States in the world adds to the president's considerable power in foreign affairs. This preeminence comes at a cost, though. Even if the president has little interest in foreign affairs, he will find much of his time and attention focused on unexpected crises emerging overseas. The economic and military power of the United States, while helping presidents enact their goals, is also a burden; presidents cannot ignore the rest of the world.

Several key themes unify this discussion of presidential foreign diplomacy. First, the pendulum has generally swung away from presidents who relied on idealism (a focus on what's best) as the underlying principle of diplomacy to those who have acted with a steady dose of pragmatism (a focus on what is possible). For example, Woodrow Wilson was unwilling to compromise on his hope of creating a "safe and just world" through the establishment of the League of Nations, while later presidents—including Franklin Roosevelt and John F. Kennedy—resolved international crises by tempering their decisions with a measure of pragmatism.

▲ Headquarters of the United Nations, New York, 1992. (Corel)

INTRODUCTION Resolving International Crises

▲ The opening session of the League of Nations in Geneva, Switzerland on November 15, 1920. The League of Nations was organized to prevent future conflicts among member states through arbitration, promotion of disarmament, and cooperation between nations. (Corel)

Second, foreign negotiating has evolved into more fluid diplomacy since the early twentieth century. Prior to Wilson's efforts during World War I, most U.S. presidents acted unilaterally in pursuing their goals in peace negotiations following war. Despite an overall shift to greater transparency in diplomacy, however, there are still instances of covert negotiations, such as the Iran-Contra scandal of the mid-1980s.

Third, public opinion has increasingly informed foreign policy. At the turn of the twentieth century, public opinion began to grow in importance as the American press circulated accounts of Spanish atrocities during the Spanish-American War to build support for McKinley and the United States. At the close of World War I, Wilson tried to garner public support for the League of Nations in his historic fall league tour. With the advent of television, the role of public opinion in foreign diplomacy became particularly vital; the public consciousness in

INTRODUCTION Resolving International Crises

▲ President Woodrow Wilson addresses a crowd of fifty thousand people on September 26, 1919, during a League of Nations peace tour. Wilson was instrumental in the creation of the organization. (Library of Congress)

opposition to the Vietnam War, for example, grew in ways unknown prior to the 1960s.

All of our presidents have faced international crises of one sort or another. In the early course of American foreign diplomacy, U.S. presidents rarely sought out advice beyond their inner circle. Presidents like James K. Polk, William McKinley, and Theodore Roosevelt made decisions informed primarily by their view of what was best for the American people. For that matter, Roosevelt's decision-making style became known as "big stick diplomacy" because of his emphasis on U.S. dominance.

Similar to these early cases, Wilson was very much an idealist, striving to create a community of nations in the ashes of World War I that would deliberate instead of fight and that would

INTRODUCTION Resolving International Crises

substitute justice for revenge. He remained steadfast in his idealistic beliefs, refusing to compromise with American allies who wanted reparations from Germany or with members of Congress who did not want the United States to give up some of its power to a League of Nations, but his stubbornness led to the loss of much of what he fought for. Conversely, Franklin Roosevelt was notably pragmatic in his negotiations with America's allies near the end of World War II. During intense negotiations at Yalta, Roosevelt made numerous accommodations to the

▼ British prime minister Winston Churchill, U.S. president Franklin D. Roosevelt, and Soviet premier Joseph Stalin at the Yalta Conference in February 1945. (National Archives and Records Administration)

INTRODUCTION Resolving International Crises

▲ President Lyndon B. Johnson greets American troops in Vietnam in 1966. (National Archives and Records Administration)

Soviet Union's Joseph Stalin in exchange for Stalin's assistance in the war effort. Roosevelt was criticized heavily by his political opponents in the United States for making deals with Stalin, but to Roosevelt, defeating Hitler was the overriding concern. The "Throughout History" section of this book contains more information on Wilson's and Roosevelt's efforts.

When presidents act pragmatically in foreign affairs, they often consider the role of public opinion. This is no mere exercise of vanity. Regardless of what the president believes would be best for the nation, he knows that the public will not support a long, bloody conflict if they do not see it as essential, and that declining public support can sharply limit the president's ability to carry out a policy. For example, President Lyndon Johnson's decision to forgo reelection was significantly affected by the growing opposition to U.S. participation in the Vietnam War. Despite

INTRODUCTION Resolving International Crises

▲ President Richard Nixon meets with Chinese Communist Party Chairman Mao Zedong during his historic 1972 China trip. (National Archives and Records Administration)

his sweeping reforms in health care, poverty, and civil rights, Johnson's legacy is often clouded by his role in the Vietnam War, a war that he inherited and dramatically escalated. He would not compromise on that war because he did not want his country, his party, or himself to look weak. The war nonetheless consumed his presidency, and he chose to retire in 1968 rather than face an election he likely would have lost.

Johnson's successor, Richard Nixon, took a very different approach to governing. Assuming that his legacy would be made by foreign affairs, he largely capitulated to congressional

INTRODUCTION Resolving International Crises

Democrats on domestic policy. Nixon's domestic achievements, including civil rights legislation and the creation of the Environmental Protection Agency, were unusual for a Republican president and reflected Nixon's willingness to compromise with Democrats on a wide range of issues. Nixon focused much of his energy on foreign policy—specifically, bringing an end to the Vietnam War and reaching out diplomatically to communist China. While his domestic policies are little remembered, Nixon's creative approach to Cold War politics is often praised by both parties today. Had it not been for his abuse of powers and subsequent resignation during the Watergate scandal, Nixon would likely be remembered as a hero of his era.

The presidencies of Johnson and Nixon illuminate not only the importance of foreign affairs to a president's job but also the tension between pragmatism and idealism. In their time, the primary objective of presidents was to oppose communism. Johnson did so in an absolutist sense, interpreting communist North Vietnam as unacceptable. He spent billions of dollars and sent thousands of American soldiers to a country that many have argued had little economic or strategic importance to the United States. Nixon, who had been obsessed with purging the United States of communists in his early congressional career, chose to reach out to one communist foe (China) in order to oppose another (the Soviet Union). Such an approach toward China reflected a good deal of pragmatism on Nixon's part and helped to build an alliance with a powerful partner while splitting the communist world.

Despite its influence, the role of public opinion in foreign policy making is never a constant one. Often, the public is not paying attention to foreign policy problems. At such times, the president is freer to act (or to not act) on a crisis. If, however, the public is paying attention, presidents will often find themselves compelled to act and to do so in a way that minimizes risk to American soldiers, even if that is not the most effective way to resolve the crisis. For example, when Ethiopia—then under a Marxist government—endured a serious famine in the early 1980s, President Reagan initially chose not to act, believing that any American aid would only help to prop up a communist state yet would be unlikely to reach the hungry. This changed when the news media and the entertainment industry began to focus on the Ethiopian famine, causing the public to take notice.

▲ Drought victims in the Bati region of Ethiopia. The African country suffered a devastating famine in 1984 and 1985 as a result of drought that decimated crops. (Corel)

INTRODUCTION Resolving International Crises

Reagan quickly reversed himself and the American government sent aid until the public's eye wandered to another issue.

This resource book will examine presidential approaches to foreign policy during wartime. It will look at the ongoing tension between pragmatism and idealism, the gap between unilateralism and diplomacy, and the role of Congress and the American public. Finally, this book will examine the ways in which presidencies have been made or broken by foreign affairs.

Sources

Thomas Knecht and Stephen Weatherford, "Public Opinion and Foreign Policy: The Stages of Presidential Decision-making," *International Studies Quarterly*, 50 (2006): 509–731.

Clifford Paterson, Maddock, Kisatsky, and Hagan, *American Foreign Relations: A History*, vol. 2, 6th ed. (Boston: Houghton Mifflin, 2005).

(Arthur Rothstein/Corbis)

THROUGHOUT HISTORY

From 1787 to Today

THROUGHOUT HISTORY

From 1787 to Today

AUTHOR

Seth Masket
University of Denver

Throughout U.S. history, presidents have faced many international crises and dealt with them in diverse ways. Some have preferred military actions over diplomatic ones, some have been guided by idealistic principles, and others have weighed their options pragmatically. Public opinion has always played a role in foreign policy decisions, and in recent times its influence has increased and thus placed greater restrictions on presidential courses of action. Developments in the twentieth century also contributed to the role of diplomacy in resolving international conflicts, further reshaping how presidents balance conflict and compromise.

The Constitution and George Washington

The history of how presidents handle international crises is rooted in the nation's founding and was shaped by both the powers delineated by the Constitution and the precedents set by the nation's first president, George Washington.

In drafting the Constitution, the founders divided war powers between the executive and legislative branches. Article I, Section 8, places the authority "to declare war" and "to raise and support armies" solely in the hands of Congress, while Article II, Section 2, names the president "commander in chief" of the armed forces. The war powers clauses are relatively vague and open to interpretation, and this ambiguity has resulted in a long-standing (and ongoing) tension between Congress and the executive. For example, presidents have often initiated wars by using their authority as commander in chief to deploy troops without a declaration of war; in fact, the last time the United States formally declared war was World War II. Conversely, Congress has fought to reassert its authority over military matters through such legislation as the 1973 War Powers Resolution.

In the wake of the American Revolution, keeping the United States out of war was central to Washington's foreign policy. In particular, he feared that involvement in European affairs could entangle the United States in drawn-out conflicts that would not benefit the emerging nation. Consequently, Washington

THROUGHOUT HISTORY From 1787 to Today

▲ The U.S. Constitution is signed on September 17, 1787, at the Constitutional Convention in Philadelphia. (Library of Congress)

issued the Proclamation of Neutrality on April 22, 1793, declaring that the United States would remain neutral during the French Revolutionary Wars. Shortly before leaving office, Washington also offered a specific warning against foreign entanglements in his September 1796 farewell address. His actions set a precedent for U.S. isolationism that was often adhered to up to World War II.

Conflict in the Nineteenth Century

By the dawn of the twentieth century, new developments in weapons technology had substantially raised the stakes for the use of military action to resolve conflicts. The development of twentieth-century mass communication provided the general public with an almost immediate awareness of domestic and world events (including graphic images of war) that contributed to the growth of popular antiwar movements. Moreover, the transmission of public opinion would have a heightened influence over the actions of political leaders. However, in the absence of such considerations in the nineteenth century, presidents enjoyed a much freer hand in making foreign policy decisions.

For example, influenced by the prevailing sentiment of manifest destiny, President James K. Polk acted unilaterally in deciding to engage in the Mexican-American War. Growing tired of stalemated negotiations with Mexico over the U.S. bid to purchase California and New Mexico in 1846, Polk ordered an army to deploy along the border in a show of force. He had already decided to use force to settle the conflict, and the outbreak of several border skirmishes provided him with the opportunity he needed to declare war.

In the absence of a widespread dissemination of firsthand reports regarding who had initiated the skirmishes, Congress—and the American public in general—were left to take Polk's word when he claimed that Mexico had "invaded our territory and shed American blood upon the American soil." Congress obliged Polk's request for a declaration of war on May 13, 1846. Despite a vocal minority who had opposed U.S. participation in the war, including Representative Abraham Lincoln and writer Henry David Thoreau, the overriding belief in manifest destiny supported Polk's course of action. Regardless of how Polk achieved his goal of territorial expansion, the majority of the American public supported and desired the end result.

As the United States spread its borders all the way to the Pacific Coast, popular sentiments of manifest destiny gave way to those of imperialism toward the end of the nineteenth century. Within that context, President William McKinley launched the Spanish-American War in 1898 under the false pretense that Spain was responsible for the explosion that sank the U.S.

▲ James Knox Polk, eleventh president of the United States (1845–1849). (Library of Congress)

THROUGHOUT HISTORY From 1787 to Today

▲ An artist's depiction of a group on a hotel porch reacting to news of the Mexican-American War. (Library of Congress)

▲ The decorated wreck of the USS *Maine* in Havana Harbor, Cuba, photographed on May 30, 1902. The USS *Maine* was sunk in Havana Harbor on February 15, 1898, increasing hostilities between the United States and Spain that eventually led to war in 1898. (Library of Congress)

battleship *Maine* in Havana harbor. The press seized the opportunity to strengthen calls for imperialism as widely exaggerated claims of Spanish atrocities inflamed the American public to support McKinley's actions. Moreover, romantic notions of war were still prominent among the public at that time, in part because exposure to graphic images of war remained limited. All these factors allowed McKinley to opt for war without facing the likelihood of widespread antiwar resistance.

The Twentieth Century: A Changing World

During the twentieth century, a dramatic shift in presidential foreign policy occurred. The rationale for the unilateral use of force and the rigid employment of idealism to resolve conflicts was supplanted by an increased need for diplomacy and compromise.

World War I marked a new era in warfare as modern weaponry and the emergence of total war wrought death and destruction on a scale never before witnessed in history. Despite the changes in modern warfare, President Woodrow Wilson's actions reflected the vestiges of moral idealism in foreign policy. Noted in his Fourteen Points Plan, Wilson was inspired to create a just and peaceful postwar world through free trade, an end to colonialism, and the creation of the League of Nations, a deliberative body that would help the peoples of Europe achieve some level of independence.

Though his league proposal was ultimately accepted by the Allies at Versailles, Wilson faced opposition at home. Following Washington's isolationist principles, Republican senators raised concerns about the obligations of the United States under the proposed league, fearing that it would force the United States to relinquish a degree of control over when and where it would send its soldiers to fight.

In late 1919, the Senate Foreign Relations Committee, under the leadership of Henry Cabot Lodge, proposed a series of fourteen amendments to the League charter, which Wilson promptly rejected. After unsuccessful negotiations with other senators, Wilson determined that his best chance of success lay in drumming up public support for the League of Nations. The public became effectively engaged in foreign policy making; however, Wilson failed to convince the Senate to support his vision. The Republican takeover

▶ Interior of the Palace des Glaces during the signing of the Peace Terms in Versailles, France on June 26, 1919. (National Archives and Records Administration)

▼ Henry Cabot Lodge was originally an isolationist, but in the years following World War I he became a proponent of American internationalism. (Perry-Castaneda Library)

of the White House in 1920 was seen as a final repudiation of Wilson's plans.

No doubt aware of Wilson's failures, President Franklin D. Roosevelt took a more pragmatic approach to foreign policy. Near the end of World War II, in February 1945, Roosevelt met with his two main allies, British prime minister Winston Churchill and Soviet premier Joseph Stalin, near Yalta on Ukraine's Crimean Peninsula. This meeting took place just weeks after the Battle of the Bulge in Belgium, where German forces had fought fiercely and inflicted many casualties on the Allies. The war had since turned in the Allies' favor, but it was far from over, and the Big Three recognized that cooperation was still necessary for victory.

▲ President Franklin D. Roosevelt and British prime minister Winston Churchill discuss politics in Quebec in 1943. (Arthur Rothstein/Corbis)

Each of the Big Three had different goals at the meeting: The Soviets sought reparations from Germany and increased influence over Poland and parts of Asia. The British sought to protect Poland from the Soviets. The Americans wanted to construct a United Nations and for the Soviets to declare war on Japan. Ultimately, Churchill and Roosevelt largely relented on Poland—Soviet-aligned communists would run Poland after the war. In exchange, Stalin pledged to declare war on Japan after Germany's surrender, and Roosevelt received support for his UN proposal.

At Yalta, Roosevelt was aware of the political realities of the day; Soviet soldiers already occupied Poland and much of Eastern

▲ Fidel Castro, prime minister (1959–1976) and president (1976–) of Cuba. (Library of Congress)

Europe, and American opposition to their presence could have led to a massive new war as the last one was winding down. He therefore opted to compromise with Stalin in order to achieve Soviet cooperation on the issues that were deemed most important.

In January 1961, President John F. Kennedy, facing an international crisis, would withstand the ultimate test in foreign policy—the Cuban Missile Crisis. Following the failed Bay of Pigs invasion, the U.S. government sponsored several futile efforts to assassinate Cuban leader Fidel Castro and undermine his regime. As a result, Castro welcomed military shipments from the Soviet Union. In October 1962, American spy planes caught images of Soviet medium-range nuclear missile launchers being built on Cuban soil. Considerations of how to respond to the crisis were complicated in a way not experienced by presidents before the rise of the nuclear age.

Several different solutions arose to address the threat of nuclear war. An air attack of the Cuban missile platforms was rejected as it might trigger Soviet reprisals. Instead, Kennedy favored a naval blockade of Cuba to prevent Soviet missiles from arriving on Cuban shores. Secret negotiations resulted in the Soviets' agreeing to dismantle their Cuban missiles in exchange for a pledge that the United States would not invade Cuba and would remove its nuclear missiles from Turkey. Because of a cautious show of force and creative diplomacy—and an interesting blend of principle and pragmatism—the United States avoided a full-scale nuclear war.

The Vietnam War marked a change in the role of public opinion in U.S. foreign affairs, and it also opened an important chapter in the ongoing tension between the legislative and executive branches with respect to conducting war abroad. The two world wars and the threat of nuclear holocaust posed by the Cold War had already given birth to a growing world peace movement by the time the Vietnam War was in full swing. Within that context, a widespread antiwar movement developed in the United States in the 1960s aimed directly at ending U.S. involvement in Vietnam.

A new development in mass communications—television—fueled antiwar sentiment by bringing images of the war directly into American homes. Unlike the reporting of earlier conflicts, television news coverage was more immediate and visual. Its powerful impact on viewers helped contribute to the antiwar

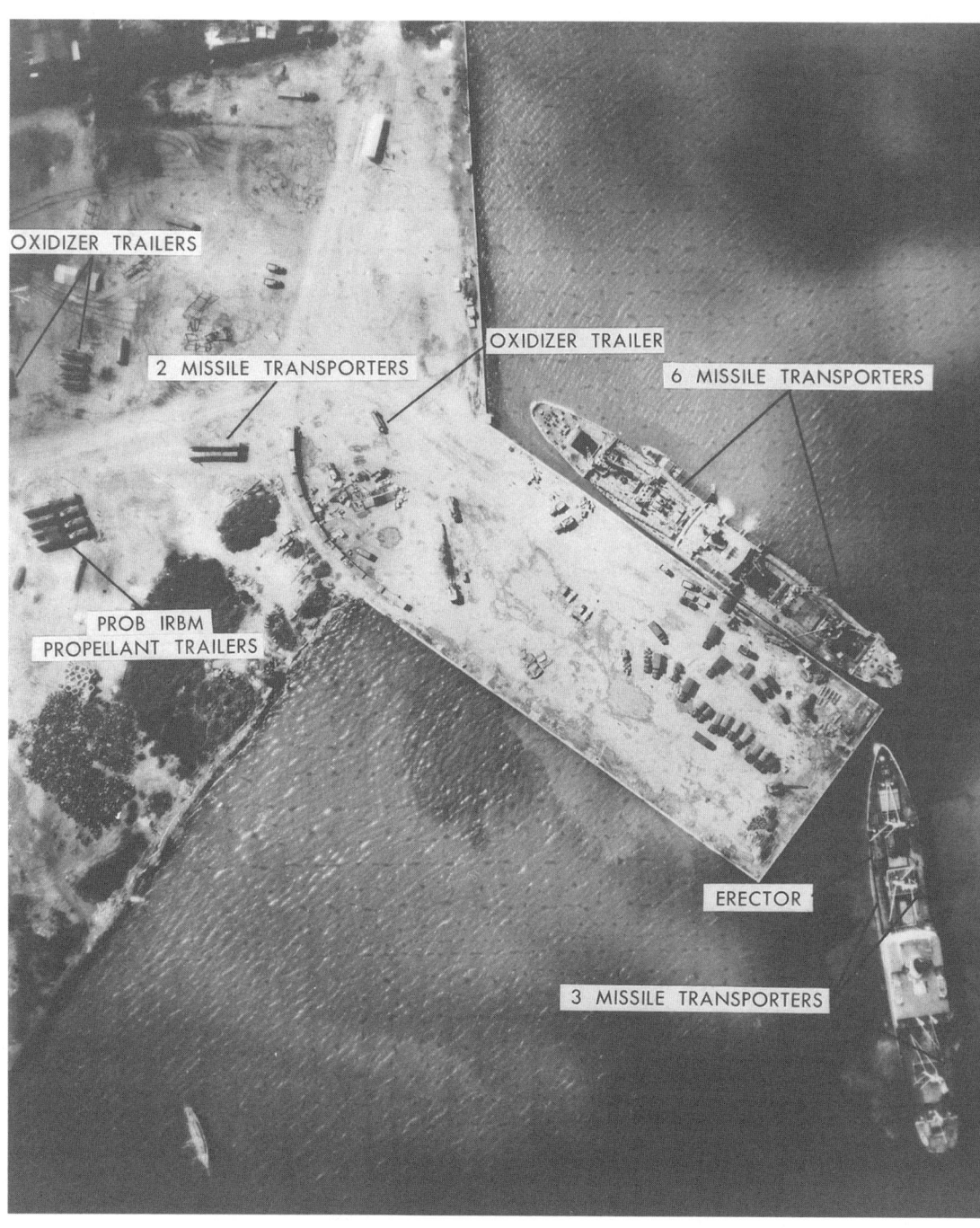

▲ View from U.S. reconnaissance aircraft of Mariel Bay, Cuba. In October of 1962, Soviet missile equipment and transport ships were photographed by U.S. U-2 spy planes, leading to the Cuban Missile Crisis. (Library of Congress)

THROUGHOUT HISTORY From 1787 to Today

▲ Vietnam War protesters, including Coretta Scott King and Dr. Benjamin Spock, crowd the White House gates on May 17, 1967. (Lyndon Baines Johnson Library and Museum)

movement. Upon taking office, President Richard Nixon was fully aware that any escalation in the war would carry serious repercussions to a nation consumed by ongoing social unrest. Nixon had also inherited an undeclared war and was limited in his actions by a Congress unwilling to give the president a blank check to deal with the crisis.

Deciding that escalation was needed to end the war, Nixon attempted to act unilaterally by ordering the secret bombing of enemy supply lines in Cambodia. News of the bombings eventually leaked to the press, inflaming the public as Nixon had feared and contributing to his downfall. Congress responded by passing the War Powers Resolution in 1973, which placed new limitations on presidential war powers, including a provision requiring the president to report to Congress any deployment of U.S. troops "into hostilities or into situations where imminent involvement in

THROUGHOUT HISTORY From 1787 to Today

▲ Richard Nixon boards a helicopter after resigning the presidency on August 9, 1974. (National Archives and Records Administration)

THROUGHOUT HISTORY From 1787 to Today

hostilities is clearly indicated by the circumstances." The resolution also required the president to withdraw troops within sixty days if Congress did not officially authorize the action. Though the resolution offered some clarification on the war powers vested by the Constitution, presidents and Congress have continued to clash over its interpretation.

Conflict and Compromise throughout U.S. History

As individuals, presidents come to different conclusions regarding how best to resolve international conflicts. Though their authority was limited by Congress, presidents in the nineteenth century had fewer considerations to weigh when confronted with crises, and thus were often more free to pursue their own desired courses of action.

Twentieth-century presidents were often more limited in foreign policy because of the emergence of new considerations in a dramatically changing world. Wilson, for example, understood the importance and power of public opinion but failed in his attempt to bring the United States into the League of Nations. Moreover, he failed to achieve his primary goal because he would not abandon his idealism and reach a compromise. Roosevelt understood that the changing nature of warfare made diplomacy and especially compromise crucial elements in resolving global conflicts. This was also true for Kennedy who, in contrast to Polk and McKinley, was president in a world greatly changed by the emergence of nuclear weapons and was compelled to rely on diplomacy rather than military action. Nixon's actions during the Vietnam War clearly demonstrated the possible consequences of acting unilaterally in foreign conflicts.

The emergence of total war, the nuclear age, and the expanded influence of public opinion are among many factors in the twentieth century that increased both the complexity of considerations and the necessity of diplomacy and compromise when presidents face international conflicts and crises. As warfare, technology, society, politics, and the nature of conflicts continue to evolve, the complexity of crises faced by presidents will likely increase and further shape how they manage conflict and compromise.

▼ President George H. W. Bush, in office from 1989 to 1993, meets with his Cabinet under the scrutiny of the media. (George Bush Library)

23

(Bettmann/Corbis)

DEFINING MOMENT I

President Wilson and the League of Nations

Introduction 26

Classroom Activities 28

Primary and Secondary Sources 46

Background Material 64

INTRODUCTION

President Wilson and the League of Nations

Until 1917, President Woodrow Wilson maintained an isolationist position of noninvolvement in World War I. That began to change after Germany stepped up acts of aggression at sea and in secret negotiations with Mexico. If Wilson could not maintain neutrality in the war, then he vowed to make the world a better place by reforming the way European countries dealt with foreign affairs. Wilson delivered his famous "Fourteen Points" speech on January 8, 1918, expressing his hopes of engineering a new mode of foreign diplomacy through more open communications and by enabling all countries to self-govern with the assistance of an international body. To help nations become independent, Wilson introduced the concept of a League of Nations, or as he put it, "a general association of nations must be formed under specific covenants for the purpose of affording mutual guarantees of political independence and territorial integrity to great and small states alike."

Wilson arrived in France in December 1918 to begin drafting a League of Nations Covenant, which promised to create more fluid international negotiations by outlawing economic barriers to trade, reducing armaments, and establishing a deliberative body to address international crises through diplomacy instead of war. In particular, Clause 10 stated that all countries participating in the league would "undertake to respect and preserve as against external aggression the territorial integrity and existing political independence of all Members of the League." After drafting the covenant, Wilson returned to the United States to seek Congressional support of the league. Senator Henry Cabot Lodge felt that Clause 10 compromised the ability of the United States to act unilaterally, and in bitter disagreement stated, "I have loved but one flag and I cannot share that devotion and give affection to the mongrel banner invented for a league."

Wilson returned to Paris to continue treaty negotiations. Provisions of the peace treaty included new boundaries for France, Belgium, and Poland; a clause requiring the assumption of "war guilt" by Germany and levying stiff war reparations against that

INTRODUCTION President Wilson and the League of Nations

nation; and the establishment of the League of Nations. Wilson thought that the heavy penalties placed on Germany worked against the ideals of the league and might make Germany more prone to take future military action. Nevertheless, with an agreement to a gradual demilitarization of Germany and an eventual transference of the Saar region to France, Wilson pledged his support for the Treaty of Versailles. Wilson had made concessions to France and Great Britain on Germany, but he refused to allow any changes to be made to the league covenant.

In July, Wilson returned to the United States seeking Senate confirmation of the treaty. It became immediately clear that the Senate was unwilling to accept the League of Nations. Much of the animosity arose from Wilson's failure to include the Senate Foreign Relations Committee in the Paris Peace Conference proceedings. Lodge and others felt that Wilson's actions contradicted his message of open negotiations; only Wilson's secretary of state, Robert Lansing, had been consulted.

With the Senate rejecting Wilson's cherished League of Nations, the president decided to take his signature plan to the American people. Wilson barnstormed across the United States on a whirlwind League of Nations tour throughout the month of September. Thoroughly exhausted, he suffered a stroke shortly after returning to Washington, D.C., and served out the rest of his term with the aid of his wife, Edith.

After continued debate, the Senate rejected the League of Nations Covenant because it would strip the United States of its role as a major world power and force the nation to act as a watchdog policing the behavior of member countries. Lodge forwarded fourteen reservations, suggesting a rejection of the treaty unless the United States would not be bound to act in defense of other member countries. The Senate ultimately voted to reject the Treaty of Versailles, and thus the league, on March 19, 1920. With the election of President Warren Harding in 1920, separate treaties would be forged with Germany, Austria, and Hungary in late 1921.

CLASSROOM ACTIVITIES

President Wilson and the League of Nations

AUTHOR

Chris Mullin
*Santa Ynez Valley
Union High School*

AUTHOR

Brett Piersma
*Santa Ynez Valley
Union High School*

In this series of document-based lessons, students will investigate various visual and written primary sources to learn about Wilson's battle for the League of Nations with Senators Lodge, Borah, and Johnson. Students will become historical detectives, learning to ask and answer both factual and thematic questions before unveiling the whole story of the conflict between the president and the Senate in 1919. Each lesson will serve as a funnel to bring the students closer to understanding the historical event.

Lesson 1 Students will conduct a dramatic reading, analyze a photograph, and study political cartoons to start their investigation of the events of 1919.

Lesson 2 Through additional document analysis, students will study the issues surrounding the League of Nations debate.

Lesson 3 Students will role play a senate subcommittee debate and vote on recommended courses of action.

CLASSROOM ACTIVITIES President Wilson and the League of Nations

Lesson 1
Anticipatory Set

MATERIALS NEEDED

For this portion of the lesson, students will need

STUDENT HANDOUT
- Cartoon Analysis Worksheet, pp. 31–32

QUOTES
- 1: from President Woodrow Wilson, p. 47
- 2: from Senator William E. Borah, p. 48

PHOTOGRAPH
- Woodrow Wilson in San Francisco, p. 49

POLITICAL CARTOONS
- "Going to Talk to the Boss," p. 50
- "Lamb from the Slaughter," p. 51
- "Refusing to Give the Lady a Seat," p. 52
- "The Gathering Storm," p. 53
- "Pilgrim Landing in America," p. 54
- "Good Subject but Must Be Remodeled," p. 55
- "Ratification Rapids," p. 56
- "Overweighted," p. 57

Before class begins, the teacher should ask two strong readers to read quotes 1 and 2. Then when class begins, the teacher can tell the students that they are about to travel through time—right into the middle of a powerful historical debate. The two students should then stand and provide dramatic readings of the quotes.

After the readings, the teacher should hold a debriefing with the class, asking students questions such as these:

- What did you hear in the two short quotes?
- Who were the speakers?
- What is the debate about?
- Who do you think will win?
- What problems did Senator Borah have with the treaty?

Note: Students will probably notice that a president and senator are involved, a treaty is being discussed, and that the treaty might lead to foreign entanglements for the United States.

After this discussion, the class should realize that a debate is occurring within the government over a treaty, though students will most likely not know much about the context of the debate. The teacher should now present another piece of evidence to help the students continue their detective work.

The teacher should project the photograph of Woodrow Wilson on a classroom screen or provide handouts to each student. This is a picture of Woodrow Wilson in San Francisco in 1919 on his tour to convince the American people to urge their senators to pass the League of Nations Covenant. The teacher should ask the students to analyze the time period in which the photograph was taken. He or she may ask questions about the type of car, styles of clothing, architecture, and other clues that might help students establish time and place.

Continues on next page

Lesson 1, continued

Now that the students have a basic understanding of the image, the teacher should probe further, asking students what questions arise when they look at this picture. The teacher might also ask how the picture might be connected to the first pair of quotations presented earlier.

The teacher can write the students' questions on the board or on poster paper, making sure not to give away too much information. This should be a time for students to begin asking questions and wondering aloud. The teacher should encourage students to keep probing.

Now that the students' interest is piqued, the teacher should tell the class that they are going to continue in the role of historical detectives by analyzing political cartoons from the year 1919. To learn what happened, students will conduct a group inquiry into history by studying these images. The teacher should inform students that the images are linked to the opening quotations and photograph and that they can apply any information or questions previously learned to the study of these new images. Each group will have a single group worksheet that will guide them through the process. Eight-person teams will compete to see which one can discover the most historical information through thoughtful analysis of images.

To begin, the teacher should divide the classroom into groups of eight students and give each group one copy of each of the political cartoons. Each student should take one of the cartoons and begin looking at the various symbols and captions. Each student should become the "expert" on his or her own cartoon document. Note: The teacher may wish to hide the captions shown below each of the images.

Once the students have studied their individual photographs, they should complete the Cartoon Analysis Worksheet as a team. The teacher should tell students to designate a group recorder who will keep the team focused and solicit feedback from each "expert." The Cartoon Analysis Worksheet gives the students an opportunity to brainstorm ideas about each individual picture while creating an overall theory about what is happening in history. The teacher should remind students that once they have finished, they will present their theory to the rest of the class.

Next, the students should present their findings to the class, one group at a time. The teacher can project the images students have been studying when they present. The teacher should tell each team that their job is to explain as well as they can what events have been taking place, when they happened, who the important figures are, and what the key issues are.

After all the groups have presented, the teacher should lead the class in a summary discussion of what they have learned as a class just by using documents.

CLASSROOM ACTIVITIES President Wilson and the League of Nations

Lesson 2
Cartoon Analysis Worksheet, Side 1

	Symbols	Captions	Questions	Possible Meaning
"Going to Talk to the Boss"				
"Lamb from the Slaughter"				
"Refusing to Give the Lady a Seat"				
"The Gathering Storm"				
"Pilgrim Landing in America"				
"Good Subject but Must Be Remodeled"				
"Ratification Rapids"				
"Overweighted"				

(See next page for Side 2, Group Task)

DEFINING MOMENT I

DEFINING MOMENT I

CLASSROOM ACTIVITIES President Wilson and the League of Nations

Lesson 2
Cartoon Analysis Worksheet, Side 2

Group Task: Now that you have analyzed these eight cartoons as a group, answer the following questions:

What events do you think the documents are portraying?

From what historical time period do these cartoons come?

What major issues or terms do you see recurring in the cartoons?

What are the names of people who reappear in these documents?

What questions about the historical events come up as you look at the cartoons?

Now write a short paragraph below describing everything you have discovered in your historical detecting and be prepared to present it to the class.

CLASSROOM ACTIVITIES President Wilson and the League of Nations

Lesson 2
Primary Source Analysis

MATERIALS NEEDED

For this portion of the lesson, students will need

LETTER
- Letter from Robert Lansing, pp. 58–59

POLITICAL CARTOONS
- "Ah Ha, My Proud Beauty, Now We Have You!," p. 60
- "The Cradle of the League of Nations," p. 61

EXCERPTS
- Article X of the League of Nations Covenant proposed by President Woodrow Wilson, p. 62
- Republican Senator Henry Cabot Lodge's "Reservation to Article X," p. 63

By now the students should have discovered as a class that a peace treaty involving the League of Nations met with resistance from the U.S. Senate in the year 1919. They should also have discovered that the main "characters" are President Wilson and Senators Lodge, Borah, and Johnson. Students may also have discovered that the treaty involved entanglements with foreign nations or at least burdensome commitments to other countries. Finally, they may have discovered that the president has tried to bypass Congress by going to the American people.

Now the students should read a firsthand account by President Wilson's secretary of state about the president's attempt to get the treaty ratified by the Senate. It highlights Wilson's determination not to compromise and his attempts to take the treaty to the American people. It also explains where the president went wrong. It does not say yet if the treaty was or was not ratified by the Senate.

While the teacher passes out the letter from Robert Lansing to each student, he or she should explain to the class that they will read a firsthand account of the events they have been deciphering through their documents. The students should be instructed to read aloud taking turns, stopping to clarify challenging vocabulary and concepts.

Once the students have finished reading, the teacher may ask them some or all of the following questions:

- Who is the writer of the letter?
- When is this story unfolding?
- What does the writer say are some of the causes of the president's trouble?
- Why does the president go out West?
- Do you know any more about the story than you did before?
- Can you answer any questions that you posed in the Lesson 2 worksheet?
- What new questions have arisen?
- What do you think will be the fate of the treaty in the Senate?

Continues on next page

CLASSROOM ACTIVITIES President Wilson and the League of Nations

Lesson 2, continued

Once students understand that the fate of the League was about to come to a vote in the Senate, their next task is to discover whether the Senate ratified the treaty.

The teacher should project or hand out copies of the political cartoon, "Ah Ha, My Proud Beauty, Now We Have You!" This cartoon, by J. N. Darling, appeared in 1923, well after the debate to join the League of Nations was over. The image strongly hints at the fact that the Senate refused to ratify the Treaty of Versailles by the placement of Uncle Sam hiding beneath the bed in the other room, helpless to assist the cruel treatment of the League. Historically, once the United States chose not to join the league, it became a frail entity with noble aspirations. The personifications of Hate, National Brigandage, Selfish Nationalism, and Racial Revenge represent real problems facing the League in the years before World War II.

Following are questions that can help guide the students in an analysis of the cartoon:

- Why is Uncle Sam depicted as hiding under the bed?
- Why is the League represented as a woman under attack?
- What do the labels of the men mean?
- What do you think National Brigandage, Selfish Nationalism, and Racial Revenge mean?
- Do you think the U.S. Senate ended up agreeing to join the League of Nations?

As an alternative, the teacher can project or hand out copies of the political cartoon "The Cradle of the League of Nations." In this cartoon, Uncle Woodrow Wilson sits rocking his baby (the League of Nations) in a coffin. This rather macabre political cartoon hints at the fact that the Senate refused to place America within the League and therefore denied it proper sustenance to survive. In the background are the prime ministers of England and France, David Lloyd George and Georges Clemenceau. Because America refused to join, the League never was able to develop any real international power. Note that students may incorrectly identify the men in the background as U.S. Senators such as Lodge, Borah, or Johnson.

Following are questions that can help guide the students in an analysis of the cartoon:

- Who is the man rocking the cradle?
- What is the title of the cradle?
- Why is the cradle also a coffin?
- Who are the men in the background?
- Do you think the U.S. Senate approved American participation in the League of Nations? Why? Why not?

CLASSROOM ACTIVITIES President Wilson and the League of Nations

Finally, now that the students have begun to decipher the events of 1919, the teacher should ask them to study the main issue of contention between the president and the Senate. In Article X (Article Ten) of the League of Nations Covenant, President Woodrow Wilson appears to pledge U.S. military personnel to the League for use in border conflicts between foreign member nations. Republican Senator Henry Cabot Lodge states his reservations to Article X. Had President Wilson compromised on this one issue, it is likely the Senate would have ratified Wilson's League of Nations proposal and the United States would have entered as a full member.

The teacher should project or distribute to each student a copy of Article X and Henry Cabot Lodge's reservations, explaining that Article X is only one of many articles in President Wilson's League of Nations proposals but is the central point of conflict over the ratification.

Students will read Article X and write down a summary of its meaning. The language is challenging, so it may be helpful to do this as a class. Students should realize that the language of the document suggests that members of the League of Nations will all stand up for each other if one or another is a victim of military aggression. It does not, however, say anything specifically about how a nation will stand up for its fellow League members.

Next, students will read Lodge's Reservations to Article X. Once again, the language is challenging and it may be helpful to do this as a class. The teacher should ask the students to write down a summary of Lodge's main changes to the original statement by Wilson. (Lodge essentially states that America should contribute no military personnel automatically to assist League members but rather will consult Congress. It was on this point primarily that Wilson refused to compromise.)

To wrap up, the teacher should engage the class in a short debriefing of the analysis of their two documents, asking the students to summarize verbally what President Wilson wanted and how Senator Lodge wanted to amend the article.

CLASSROOM ACTIVITIES President Wilson and the League of Nations

Lesson 3
Senate Subcommittee Debate

MATERIALS NEEDED

For this portion of the lesson, students will need

ROLE CARDS WITH EXCERPTS FROM SPEECHES
- A: Senator Jackson's Role Card with President Woodrow Wilson's 1919 Excerpt, p. 38
- B: Senator Tyler's Role Card with President Woodrow Wilson's 1919 Excerpt, p. 39
- C: Senator Graham's Role Card with Henry Cabot Lodge's 1919 Excerpt, p. 40
- D: Senator Johnson's Role Card with Henry Cabot Lodge's 1919 Excerpt, p. 41
- E: Senator Taft's Role Card with Henry Cabot Lodge's 1919 Excerpt, p. 42
- F: Senator Parker's Role Card with Henry Cabot Lodge's 1919 Excerpt, p. 43
- G: Senator Wilkes's Role Card with Henry Cabot Lodge's "The League of Nations Must Be Revised" Excerpt, p. 44
- H: Senator Harper's Role Card with Henry Cabot Lodge's "The League of Nations Must Be Revised" Excerpt, p. 45

Now that the students are beginning to weave together a picture of the 1919 events surrounding the Treaty of Versailles, they are each going to play the role of a U.S. senator in a subcommittee debate. In order to complete this task, each student will receive a role card with a primary source that expresses an opinion related to Article X and the proposed American commitments in Europe. The number of role cards for and against will deliberately be divided unevenly so that the senators favoring amendment will win.

First, the teacher should divide the class into teams of eight and give each team the eight role/primary source cards. Students should each read one personal profile and short primary source secretly to themselves, then write a short 50–100 word statement in which they combine:

CLASSROOM ACTIVITIES President Wilson and the League of Nations

A. Key phrases from their own role card and primary source document.

B. The overall point of view of their primary source for or against Article X.

C. A clearly stated position relating to whether he wishes to accept or amend Article X.

Following this exercise, the students should now be ready to engage in a debate over the following question:

Should the United States Senate vote to accept or amend Article X of President Wilson's proposal for a League of Nations?

The teacher should arrange for one student to be a moderator in each group, whether by appointment or group election. Once every "senator" has completed his or her position statement, the moderator should call on all committee members to read their short statements.

Once all statements have been read (including the moderator's), the moderator should lead the group in a more informal debate over the primary question. Each student should remain firm and try to successfully accomplish the agenda of his or her role card. When all debating has come to an end, the moderator should call for a vote by a show of hands on the question.

After all groups have voted, the teacher should bring the students back to their regular seats and debrief the results of the individual elections.

CLASSROOM ACTIVITIES President Wilson and the League of Nations

Lesson 3
Role Card A

Senatorial Role
Senator Jackson

Related Document
President Woodrow Wilson 1919 Excerpt

Senator Jackson (Democrat)
You believe that it is critical that Article X passes unchanged. If the League of Nations is going to have any power to do good in Europe, it must be able to rely on the promise of American force. Without Article X, Europe will not believe in America's commitment to the process of creating a new world order of democracy and security.

President Woodrow Wilson (1919)
The United States will, indeed, undertake under Article X to 'respect and preserve as against external aggression the territorial integrity and existing political independence of all members of the League,' and that engagement constitutes a very grave and solemn moral obligation. But it is a moral, not a legal, obligation, and leaves our Congress absolutely free to put its own interpretation upon it in all cases that call for action. It is binding in conscience only, not in law. Article X seems to me to constitute the very backbone of the whole Covenant. Without it the League would be hardly more than an influential debating society. . . . Pardon me, Mr. Chairman, if I have been entirely unreserved and plainspoken in speaking of the great matters we all have so much at heart. If excuse is needed, I trust that the critical situation of affairs may serve as my justification. The issues that manifestly hang upon the conclusions of the Senate with regard to peace and upon the time of its action are so grave and so clearly insusceptible of being thrust on one side or postponed that I have felt it necessary in the public interest to make this urgent plea, and to make it as simply and as unreservedly as possible.

Now write a short 100-word statement in which you incorporate

    A. key phrases from the above primary source.

    B. the overall point of view of your primary source for or against Article X.

    C. a clearly stated position relating to whether he wishes to accept or amend Article X.

CLASSROOM ACTIVITIES President Wilson and the League of Nations

Lesson 3
Role Card B

Senatorial Role
Senator Tyler

Related Document
President Woodrow Wilson 1919 Excerpt

Senator Tyler (Democrat)
You believe it is critical that Article X passes unchanged. If the League of Nations is going to have any power to do good in Europe, it must be able to rely on the promise of American force. Without Article X, Europe will not believe in America's commitment to the process of creating a new world order of democracy and security.

President Woodrow Wilson (1919)
The United States would suffer the contempt of the world (with an amended Article X). We will be playing into Germany's hands. . . . If the Republicans are bent on defeating this Treaty, I want the vote of each, Republican and Democrat, recorded, because they will have to answer to the country in the future for their acts. They must answer to the people. I am a sick man, lying in this bed, but I am going to debate this issue with these gentlemen in their respective states whenever they come up for re-election if I have breath enough in my body to carry on the fight. I shall do this even if I have to give my life to it. And I will get their political scalps when the truth is known to the people. They have got to account to their constituents for their actions in this matter. I have no doubt as to what the verdict of the people will be when they know the facts.

Now write a short 100-word statement in which you incorporate

    A. key phrases from the above primary source.

    B. the overall point of view of your primary source for or against Article X.

    C. a clearly stated position relating to whether he wishes to accept or amend Article X.

CLASSROOM ACTIVITIES President Wilson and the League of Nations

Lesson 3
Role Card C

Senatorial Role
Senator Graham

Related Document
Henry Cabot Lodge's 1919 Excerpt

Senator Graham (Republican)
You believe that if Article X passes unchanged, American soldiers will forever have to do the bidding of foreign nations. You wish to amend Article X to spell out Congress's control of all military operations overseas.

Henry Cabot Lodge (1919)
I believe that we do not require to be told by foreign nations when we shall do work which freedom and civilization require. I think we can move to victory much better under our own command than under the command of others. Let us unite with the world to promote the peaceable settlement of all international disputes. Let us try to develop international law. Let us associate ourselves with the other nations for these purposes. But let us retain in our own hands and in our own control the lives of the youth of the land. Let no American be sent into battle except by the constituted authorities of his own country and by the will of the people of the United States. I have loved but one flag and I cannot share that devotion and give affection to the mongrel banner invented for a league.

Now write a short 100-word statement in which you incorporate

    A. key phrases from the above primary source.

    B. the overall point of view of your primary source for or against Article X.

    C. a clearly stated position relating to whether he wishes to accept or amend Article X.

CLASSROOM ACTIVITIES President Wilson and the League of Nations

DEFINING MOMENT I

Lesson 3
Role Card D

Senatorial Role
Senator Johnson

Related Document
Henry Cabot Lodge's 1919 Excerpt

Senator Johnson (Republican)
You believe that if Article X passes unchanged, American soldiers will forever have to do the bidding of foreign nations. You wish to amend Article X to spell out Congress's control of all military operations overseas.

Henry Cabot Lodge (1919)
The United States is the world's best hope, but if you fetter her in the interests and quarrels of other nations, if you tangle her in the intrigues of Europe, you will destroy her power for good and endanger her very existence. Leave her to march freely through the centuries to come as in the years that have gone. Strong, generous, and confident, she has nobly served mankind. Beware how you trifle with your marvelous inheritance, this great land of ordered liberty, for if we stumble and fall, freedom and civilizations everywhere will go down in ruin.

Now write a short 100-word statement in which you incorporate

    A. key phrases from the above primary source.

    B. the overall point of view of your primary source for or against Article X.

    C. a clearly stated position relating to whether he wishes to accept or amend Article X.

CLASSROOM ACTIVITIES President Wilson and the League of Nations

Lesson 3
Role Card E

Senatorial Role
Senator Taft

Related Document
Henry Cabot Lodge's 1919 Excerpt

Senator Taft (Republican)
You believe that if Article X passes unchanged, American soldiers will forever have to do the bidding of foreign nations. You wish to amend Article X to spell out Congress's control of all military operations overseas.

Henry Cabot Lodge (1919)
As it stands there is no doubt whatever in my mind that American troops and American ships may be ordered to any part of the world by nations other than the United States, and that is a proposition to which I for one can never assent. It must be made perfectly clear that no American soldiers, not even a corporal's guard, that no American sailors, not even the crew of a submarine, can ever be engaged in war or ordered anywhere except by the constitutional authorities of the United States. To Congress is granted by the Constitution the right to declare war, and nothing that would take the troops out of the country at the bidding or demand of other nations should ever be permitted except through congressional action. The lives of Americans must never be sacrificed except by the will of the American people expressed through their chosen Representatives in Congress. This is a point upon which no doubt can be permitted.

Now write a short 100-word statement in which you incorporate

A. key phrases from the above primary source.

B. the overall point of view of your primary source for or against Article X.

C. a clearly stated position relating to whether he wishes to accept or amend Article X.

CLASSROOM ACTIVITIES President Wilson and the League of Nations

Lesson 3
Role Card F

Senatorial Role
Senator Parker

Related Document
Henry Cabot Lodge's 1919 Excerpt

Senator Parker (Republican)
You believe that if Article X passes unchanged, American soldiers will forever have to do the bidding of foreign nations. You wish to amend Article X to spell out Congress's control of all military operations overseas.

Henry Cabot Lodge (1919)
American soldiers and American sailors have never failed the country when the country called upon them. They went in their hundreds of thousands into the war just closed. They went to die for the great cause of freedom and of civilization. . . . It was done by the American soldier, the American sailor, and the spirit and energy of the American people. They overrode all obstacles and all shortcomings on the part of the administration or of Congress and gave to their country a great place in the great victory. It was the first time we had been called upon to rescue the civilized world. Did we fail? On the contrary, we succeeded, succeeded largely and nobly, and we did it without any command from any league of nations. When the emergency came we met it, and we were able to meet it because we had built up on this continent the greatest and most powerful nation in the world, built it up under our own policies, in our own way, and one great element of our strength was the fact that we had held aloof and had not thrust ourselves into European quarrels; that we had no selfish interest to serve. We made great sacrifices. We have done splendid work.

Now write a short 100-word statement in which you incorporate

    A. key phrases from the above primary source.

    B. the overall point of view of your primary source for or against Article X.

    C. a clearly stated position relating to whether he wishes to accept or amend Article X.

CLASSROOM ACTIVITIES President Wilson and the League of Nations

Lesson 3
Role Card G

Senatorial Role
Senator Wilkes

Related Document
Henry Cabot Lodge's "The League of Nations Must Be Revised" Excerpt

Senator Wilkes (Republican)
You believe that if Article X passes unchanged, American soldiers will forever have to do the bidding of foreign nations. You wish to amend Article X to spell out Congress's control of all military operations overseas.

Henry Cabot Lodge: "The League of Nations Must Be Revised"

I think it is not only our right but our duty to determine how far we shall go. Not only must we look carefully to see where we are being led into endless disputes and entanglements, but we must not forget that we have in this country millions of people of foreign birth and parentage. Our one great object is to make all these people Americans so that we may call on them to place America first and serve America as they have done in the war just closed. We can not Americanize them if we are continually thrusting them back into the quarrels and difficulties of the countries from which they came to us. We shall fill this land with political disputes about the troubles and quarrels of other countries. We shall have a large portion of our people voting not on American questions and not on what concerns the United States but dividing on issues which concern foreign countries alone. That is an unwholesome and perilous condition to force upon this country. We must avoid it. We ought to reduce to the lowest possible point the foreign questions in which we involve ourselves.

Now write a short 100-word statement in which you incorporate

    A. key phrases from the above primary source.

    B. the overall point of view of your primary source for or against Article X.

    C. a clearly stated position relating to whether he wishes to accept or amend Article X.

CLASSROOM ACTIVITIES President Wilson and the League of Nations

Lesson 3
Role Card H

Senatorial Role
Senator Harper

Related Document
Henry Cabot Lodge's "The League of Nations Must Be Revised" Excerpt

Senator Harper (Republican)
You believe that if Article X passes unchanged, American soldiers will forever have to do the bidding of foreign nations. You wish to amend Article X to spell out Congress's control of all military operations overseas.

Henry Cabot Lodge: "The League of Nations Must Be Revised"
Never forget that this league is primarily—I might say overwhelmingly—a political organization, and I object strongly to having the policies of the United States turn upon disputes where deep feeling is aroused but in which we have no direct interest. It will all tend to delay the Americanization of our great population, and it is more important not only to the United States but to the peace of the world to make all these people good Americans than it is to determine that some piece of territory should belong to one European country rather than to another. For this reason I wish to limit strictly our interference in the affairs of Europe and of Africa. We have interests of our own in Asia and in the Pacific which we must guard upon our own account, but the less we undertake to play the part of umpire and thrust ourselves into European conflicts the better for the United States and for the world.

Now write a short 100-word statement in which you incorporate

    A. key phrases from the above primary source.

    B. the overall point of view of your primary source for or against Article X.

    C. a clearly stated position relating to whether he wishes to accept or amend Article X.

PRIMARY AND SECONDARY SOURCES

President Wilson and the League of Nations

SOURCES President Wilson and the League of Nations

Lesson 1 Quote
Quote 1

Quote from President Woodrow Wilson

Either we should enter the League fearlessly, accepting with responsibility and not fearing the role of leadership which we now enjoy, contributing our efforts toward establishing a just and permanent peace, or we should retire as gracefully as possible from the great concert of powers by which the world was saved.

President Woodrow Wilson

Lesson 1 Quote
Quote 2

Quote from Senator William E. Borah

Entertain no compromise; have none of it. This states the position I occupy at this time and which I have, in a humble way, occupied from the first contention in regard to this proposal. My objections to the league have not been met by the reservationists. . . . Tell me where is the reservation in these articles which protects us against entangling alliances with Europe?

Senator William E. Borah

SOURCES President Wilson and the League of Nations

Lesson 1 Photograph
Woodrow Wilson in San Francisco

▲ A Secret Service agent rides on the running board of President Woodrow Wilson's automobile as President Wilson waves his hat (inside the automobile) during his League of Nations peace tour visit to San Francisco, September 1919. (Corbis)

SOURCES President Wilson and the League of Nations

Lesson 1 Political Cartoon
"Going to Talk to the Boss"

▲ A 1919 political cartoon entitled "Going to Talk to the Boss" satirizes the League of Nations. (Bettmann/Corbis)

SOURCES President Wilson and the League of Nations

Lesson 1 Political Cartoon
"Lamb from the Slaughter"

▲ A political cartoon from 1919 shows Henry Cabot Lodge, chairman of the Senate Foreign Relations Committee, escorting a battered figure on crutches ("Peace Treaty") out of a room labeled "Operating Room, Senate Committee on Foreign Relations." Conservative senators had grave concerns over the provisions of the Treaty of Versailles that ended the first World War and provided for the establishment of the League of Nations. When the Senate Foreign Relations Committee finally reported the treaty to the full Senate on September 10, they included forty-five amendments and reservations. President Wilson refused to accept any of the reservations and the treaty was eventually rejected on November 19, 1919. (Library of Congress)

SOURCES President Wilson and the League of Nations

Lesson 1 Political Cartoon
"Refusing to Give the Lady a Seat"

▲ Political cartoon depicts Senators William Borah, Henry Cabot Lodge, and Hiram Johnson refusing a seat to "Peace," circa 1919. These senators and other Republican isolationists lobbied against ratification of the Treaty of Versailles and U.S. involvement in the League of Nations, a move that this cartoonist felt would threaten the establishment of peace following World War I. (Library of Congress)

SOURCES President Wilson and the League of Nations

Lesson 1 Political Cartoon
"The Gathering Storm"

▲ "The Gathering Storm" cartoon suggests that public sentiment supporting American involvement in the League of Nations will prevail over Senator Henry Cabot Lodge's opposition to joining the League. (Library of Congress)

SOURCES President Wilson and the League of Nations

Lesson 1 Political Cartoon
"Pilgrim Landing in America"

▲ Wilson's League of Nations proposal returns unfriendly Republican reception in this political cartoon entitled "Pilgrim Landing in America," printed in the *Brooklyn Daily Eagle* in 1919. (*Brooklyn Daily Eagle*)

SOURCES President Wilson and the League of Nations

Lesson 1 Political Cartoon
"Good Subject but Must Be Remodeled"

▲ A 1919 political cartoon titled "Good Subject but Must Be Remodeled" critiques the League of Nations. (Library of Congress)

SOURCES President Wilson and the League of Nations

Lesson 1 Political Cartoon
"Ratification Rapids"

▲ A 1919 cartoon depicts President Wilson trying to navigate the Treaty of Versailles through stormy rapids. (Bettmann/Corbis)

SOURCES President Wilson and the League of Nations

Lesson 1 Political Cartoon
"Overweighted"

▲ Political cartoon of Woodrow Wilson handing a small dove a huge olive branch marked "League of Nations," 1919. (Library of Congress)

DEFINING MOMENT I

SOURCES President Wilson and the League of Nations

Lesson 2 Letter

Letter from Robert Lansing, President Woodrow Wilson's Secretary of State, 1919

By the time this letter reaches you the fate of the Treaty in the Senate will have been decided and so my comments as to the . . . [probabilities] of its ratification in any form at all acceptable would be of doubtful value. . . . If his enemies could practically destroy the League or render it worthless, they were particularly desirous of doing so because they felt that it would humble his pride of authorship and prove to the world that he was by no means so great and powerful as had been supposed. With this end in view the Senate majority began its campaign apparently against the Covenant but really against the President. The earlier hearings before the Committee on Foreign Relations, among them mine, showed conclusively that it was personal hostility to the President which was the controlling motive, and that the interests of the United States were really secondary to them in importance. . . .

There is no doubt that at the outset the great majority of the people were back of the President and the League. I felt that if the President did not assume a defensive attitude he would in large measure retain this popular support, but that, if he began to explain the Covenant, he would unavoidably become involved in arguments which would be subject to attack arousing doubt as to their validity in the public mind. For that reason I strongly advised him two days after I landed, not to make a speaking tour for the League. He yielded very unwillingly agreeing to postpone his trip, though he would not abandon it. I had hoped that the postponement would result in abandonment, but as the attacks on the weak points in the Covenant increased in virulence the President became incensed and pugnacious with the result that he was inflexible in his determination to go out and appeal to the people over the heads of the Senators. . . .

SOURCES President Wilson and the League of Nations

Lesson 2 Letter

Letter from Robert Lansing, President Woodrow Wilson's Secretary of State, 1919, continued

You know, if you followed the President's speeches in the West that, while he used some rather undignified expressions about the opposition in the Senate, he sought to defend the Covenant and its various provisions. I am sure the performance lost rather than gained support for the Treaty. It came to me from various sources that the public began to consider that the objections had some merit otherwise the President would not have taken so much trouble to answer them. Prior to his western trip the public were disposed to brush the objections aside on the supposition that they were only put forward to discredit the President rather than the Treaty. Thus, the President's speeches, while they may have won over a few, lost, in my opinion, a great deal of public support, especially as the whole proceeding took on the character of a party issue.

The President lost the best chance to compromise on moderate reservations last August. I suggested that policy to him and his jaw shot out and he said that there were going to be no reservations and if the opposition wanted a fight they would "get a damned good one," referring of course to his appeal to the people.

SOURCES President Wilson and the League of Nations

Lesson 2 Political Cartoon
"Ah Ha, My Proud Beauty, Now We Have You!"

▲ J. N. "Ding" Darling's "Ah Ha, My Proud Beauty, Now We Have You!" political cartoon, published September 9, 1923. ("Ding" Darling Wildlife Society)

SOURCES President Wilson and the League of Nations

Lesson 2 Political Cartoon
"The Cradle of the League of Nations"

▲ "The Cradle of the League of Nations," an undated political cartoon, depicts Woodrow Wilson rocking a cradle that is a coffin. David Lloyd George and Georges Clemenceau are in the background. (Corbis)

Lesson 2 Excerpt
Excerpt 1

Article X of the League of Nations Covenant proposed by President Woodrow Wilson

The Members of the League undertake to respect and preserve as against external aggression the territorial integrity and existing political independence of all Members of the League. In case of any such aggression or in case of any threat or danger of such aggression the Council shall advise upon the means by which this obligation shall be fulfilled.

SOURCES President Wilson and the League of Nations

Lesson 2 Excerpt
Excerpt 2

Republican Senator Henry Cabot Lodge's "Reservation to Article X"

The United States assumed no obligation to preserve the territorial integrity or political independence of any country or to interfere in controversies between nations—whether members of the league or not—under the provisions of Article X or to employ the military or naval forces of the United States under any article of the treaty for any purpose, unless in any particular case the Congress, which, under the Constitution, has the sole power to declare war or authorize the employment of the military or naval forces of the United States, shall by act or joint resolution so provide.

BACKGROUND MATERIAL

President Wilson and the League of Nations

BACKGROUND MATERIAL President Wilson and the League of Nations

Glossary Words

collective security Collective security is an agreement among nations that an attack on one state is also an attack on all the member states. Because all the nations, not just the attacked nation, would retaliate against the attacker, proponents of collective security believe that such an agreement is a deterrent to war. The idea of collective security inspired the formation of the League of Nations and the United Nations.

Fourteen Points Germany's surrender in World War I was negotiated on the basis of America's terms for peace, set forth by U.S. president Woodrow Wilson as the Fourteen Points, which dealt with such issues as European and Turkish territorial adjustments and, most importantly for Wilson, the establishment of a general association of nations, which became the League of Nations.

isolationism Isolationism is a term that describes a foreign policy of limited involvement in the world outside the home state. It entails avoidance of political and military commitments and requires specific criteria for intervention. The most popular use of the term has been in describing U.S. foreign policy, the history of which has been widely identified as the result of tension between isolationism and intervention.

moral idealism Moral idealism is a political philosophy based on the belief that every country is equally willing to agree on and act on moral standards of behavior. The Peace Corps and the now defunct League of Nations are examples of organizations that embody this concept. Political realism is at the other end of the philosophical spectrum.

BACKGROUND MATERIAL President Wilson and the League of Nations

Biographies

▲ William Borah
(Library of Congress)

▲ Robert Lansing
(Library of Congress)

William Borah (1865–1940) A progressive Republican in the Senate, William Borah is chiefly remembered for his fierce opposition to U.S. membership in the League of Nations.

In 1919, Borah toured the nation delivering speeches in opposition to Woodrow Wilson's proposal that the United States join the League of Nations. He felt that American politics would become contaminated by exposure to the machinations and corruption of European politics. His fiery condemnation of the idea of U.S. membership in the league left no room for compromise.

When the Republicans regained control of the White House and Congress in the 1920s, Borah's power grew. From 1925 to 1933, he was chairman of the Senate Foreign Relations Committee. In this position, he supported the recognition of the Soviet Union, favored collection of World War I debts, and opposed intervention in Latin American countries to protect U.S. investments.

Robert Lansing (1864–1928) As secretary of state from 1915 to 1920, Robert Lansing attempted to play an important role balancing what he perceived to be President Woodrow Wilson's visionary idealism with political pragmatism.

Lansing helped set the stage for U.S. involvement in World War I on the side of the Allies. After several American ships had been torpedoed, it was Lansing who argued most persuasively for a declaration of war on the grounds that Germany had broken its pledge not to engage in unrestricted submarine warfare.

Lansing viewed Wilson's pledge of "peace without victory" and commitment of the United States to support the creation of a world government as unrealistic, but this did not disrupt their working relationship until after the Allied victory. Wilson asked for his resignation in 1920, shortly after Lansing publicly expressed his personal apprehensions about the extent of the proposed U.S. commitment to the League of Nations.

Henry Cabot Lodge (1850–1924) Serving as a U.S. senator for more than three decades, Lodge staunchly opposed President Woodrow Wilson's foreign policy views, especially the League of Nations. Lodge pushed for U.S. military preparedness and advocated a strong international role for the United States, including entry into World War I on the Allied side.

BACKGROUND MATERIAL President Wilson and the League of Nations

As Senate majority leader following the November 1918 election and chair of the Senate Committee on Foreign Relations from 1919, Lodge held a pivotal position in the fight against Wilson's cherished League of Nations, which became a key issue shortly after the November 1918 election and continued into March 1920. President Wilson failed to consult leading Republicans regarding the Paris Peace Conference and his proposed League of Nations, and he excluded them from membership in the U.S. delegation.

On November 6, 1919, Lodge proposed a resolution with fourteen reservations that, while somewhat circumventing U.S. obligations under the League Covenant, did not seriously impair the League. Wilson urged its defeat, and Democrats joined with the irreconcilable Republicans on November 19 to vote down the resolution 38–53. However, by March 1920, twenty-one Democrats had deserted Wilson to join Lodge, and the Senate rejected the Treaty of Versailles containing the League of Nations Covenant. Although Lodge is sometimes blamed for the failure of the United States to join the League of Nations, most historians argue that blame more properly belongs with President Wilson and his refusal to compromise.

Woodrow Wilson (1856–1924) Receiving his Ph.D. from Johns Hopkins University in 1886, Wilson spent over two decades in academia before becoming president of the United States in 1913. After the outbreak of World War I in 1914, his administration initially adopted a policy of strict neutrality. With German aggression building by mid-1915, however, the United States joined the war on April 2, 1917.

When Germany was forced to capitulate in 1918, it was Wilson who negotiated the surrender terms and then obtained Allied approval based on his famous Fourteen Points. Eight pertained to territorial adjustments; others called for open treaty negotiations, reduction of armaments, and impartial adjustment of colonial claims. The most important points to Wilson were his call for the creation of the League of Nations and the concept of self-determination.

▲ Woodrow Wilson
(Library of Congress)

Determined to be remembered as the man who established the framework for permanent peace, Wilson decided to lead the U.S. delegation to the peace conference in Paris in 1919.

BACKGROUND MATERIAL President Wilson and the League of Nations

Biographies, continued

Although Germany was forced to relinquish its colonies, virtually eliminate its armed forces, and accept a huge war reparations burden, Wilson prevented the country's dismemberment. He also played an important role in the creation of a new Poland and achieved his most cherished goal: the creation of the League of Nations.

Wilson mistakenly assumed that the U.S. Senate would approve his actions. Even after he toured the nation in a dramatic appeal for popular support that so exhausted him he suffered a debilitating stroke in October 1919, he could not secure the treaty's ratification in the Senate.

Unable to lead the debate for public support due to the paralysis caused by his stroke, Wilson nevertheless would not compromise. His refusal to discuss changes in the language of the treaty to eliminate the commitment of the United States to collective security and participation in the league resulted in a stalemate that lasted until Wilson's view was repudiated with the Republican landslide victory in the 1920 presidential election. Nevertheless, Wilson was awarded the Nobel Peace Prize in 1919 for his efforts to establish the League of Nations.

BACKGROUND MATERIAL President Wilson and the League of Nations

Organizations and Events

election of 1920 The election of 1920 was an exceedingly apathetic one. The nation was exhausted from World War I and weary of domestic reforms and debate over the League of Nations. It was said that any Republican nominee could win the election. Campaigning on a platform that promised a return to "normalcy," Ohio's Warren Harding proved the statement correct. Midterm elections in 1918 had given Republicans the majority in the House and the Senate, where they attacked President Woodrow Wilson's foreign policy, especially the League of Nations. Desiring change, the American people turned to the Republican Party.

Wilson harbored hopes of being nominated for a third term by the Democrats, but he had suffered a stroke in 1919 and was barely considered. Instead, the party nominated Governor James M. Cox of Ohio at its convention in San Francisco. The Democratic platform praised Wilson's administration and supported the League of Nations. Harding easily won the election in what political analysts termed an "election by disgust."

League of Nations The League of Nations was organized to pursue an international ideal by preventing future conflicts among its member states through arbitration and promotion of disarmament and cooperation between nations in the aftermath of World War I. President Woodrow Wilson, who had advocated the League of Nations in his famous "Fourteen Points" speech, championed the idea at the Paris Peace Conference.

Neutral states were eligible to become original members, and defeated nations were eventually permitted to join. The League of Nations was designated to oversee the activities of the Allied nations in dividing up and administering the territories of Germany and Turkey. The organization thus brought some international oversight to the actions of Britain and France as the victors defined boundaries and authority in the Middle East and parts of Africa. The League of Nations was organized with a council and assembly, prefiguring the Security Council and General Assembly that would later structure the United Nations (UN). Sixty-three countries eventually joined; the United States was the glaring holdout.

BACKGROUND MATERIAL President Wilson and the League of Nations

Excerpts from Speeches

Woodrow Wilson: "Fourteen Points" speech (1918)

1. Open covenants of peace, openly arrived at, after which there shall be no private international understandings of any kind but diplomacy shall proceed always frankly and in the public view. . . .

3. The removal, so far as possible, of all economic barriers and the establishment of an equality of trade conditions among all the nations consenting to the peace and associating themselves for its maintenance.

4. Adequate guarantees given and taken that national armaments will be reduced to the lowest point consistent with domestic safety.

5. A free, open-minded, and absolutely impartial adjustment of all colonial claims, based upon a strict observance of the principle that in determining all such questions of sovereignty the interests of the populations concerned must have equal weight with the equitable claims of the government whose title is to be determined. . . .

14. A general association of nations must be formed under specific covenants for the purpose of affording mutual guarantees of political independence and territorial integrity to great and small states alike.

Woodrow Wilson: "League of Nations" speech (1919)

Inasmuch as I am stating it in the presence of the official representatives of the various governments here present, including myself, I may say that there is a universal feeling that the world cannot rest satisfied with merely official guidance. There has reached us through many channels the feeling that if the deliberating body of the League of Nations was merely to be a body of officials representing the various governments, the peoples of the world would not be sure that some of the mistakes which preoccupied officials had admittedly made might not be repeated. . . . And you will notice that this body has unlimited rights of discussion. I mean of discussion of anything that falls within the field of international relations—and that it is especially agreed that war or international misunderstandings or anything that may lead to friction or trouble is everybody's business, because it may affect the peace of the world.

BACKGROUND MATERIAL President Wilson and the League of Nations

Henry Cabot Lodge: "Opposition to the Treaty of Versailles" speech (1919)

We were late in entering the war. We made no preparation, as we ought to have done, for the ordeal which was clearly coming upon us; but we went and we turned the wavering scale. . . . Did we fail? On the contrary, we succeeded, succeeded largely and nobly, and we did it without any command from any league of nations. When the emergency came we met it, and we were able to meet it because we had built up on this continent the greatest and most powerful nation in the world, built it up under our own policies, in our own way, and one great element of our strength was the fact that we had held aloof and had not thrust ourselves into European quarrels; . . . I have loved but one flag and I cannot share that devotion and give affection to the mongrel banner invented for a league. Internationalism, illustrated by the Bolshevik and by the men to whom all countries are alike, provided they can make money out of them, is to me repulsive.

Woodrow Wilson: annual message (1919)

The whole world gave its recognition and endorsement to these fundamental purposes in the League of Nations. The statesmen gathered at Versailles recognized the fact that world stability could not be had by reverting to industrial standards and conditions against which the average workman of the world had revolted. . . .

The establishment of the principles regarding labor laid down in the covenant of the League of Nations offers us the way to industrial peace and conciliation. No other road lies open to us. Not to pursue this one is longer to invite enmities, bitterness, and antagonisms which in the end only lead to industrial and social disaster. . . . The evidences of worldwide unrest which manifest themselves in violence throughout the world bid us pause and consider the means to be found to stop the spread of this contagious thing before it saps the very vitality of the nation itself. Do we gain strength by withholding the remedy?

Henry Cabot Lodge: quote on the League of Nations

I have loved but one flag and I can not share that devotion and give affection to the mongrel banner invented for a league. (Speech to the Senate regarding the League of Nations, August 12, 1919)

Excerpts of Official Documents

League of Nations covenant (1919) with amendments (1924)
ARTICLE X
The Members of the League undertake to respect and preserve as against external aggression the territorial integrity and existing political independence of all Members of the League. In case of any such aggression or in case of any threat or danger of such aggression the Council shall advise upon the means by which this obligation shall be fulfilled.

ARTICLE XI
Any war or threat of war, whether immediately affecting any of the Members of the League or not, is hereby declared a matter of concern to the whole League, and the League shall take any action that may be deemed wise and effectual to safeguard the peace of nations. In case any such emergency should arise the Secretary General shall on the request of any Member of the League forthwith summon a meeting of the Council.

It is also declared to be the friendly right of each Member of the League to bring to the attention of the Assembly or of the Council any circumstance whatever affecting international relations which threatens to disturb international peace or the good understanding between nations upon which peace depends.

Treaty of Versailles (1919)
THE HIGH CONTRACTING PARTIES, In order to promote international co-operation and to achieve international peace and security by the acceptance of obligations not to resort to war by the prescription of open, just and honourable relations between nations by the firm establishment of the understandings of international law as the actual rule of conduct among Governments, and by the maintenance of justice and a scrupulous respect for all treaty obligations in the dealings of organized peoples with one another Agree to this Covenant of the League of Nations.

ARTICLE X
The Members of the League undertake to respect and preserve as against external aggression the territorial integrity and existing political independence of all Members of the League. In case of any such aggression or in case of any threat or danger of such aggression the Council shall advise upon the means by which this obligation shall be fulfilled.

BACKGROUND MATERIAL President Wilson and the League of Nations

League of Nations: Report on the Japanese invasion of Manchuria (1933)

The situation which led up to the events of September 18th, 1931 . . . was subsequently aggravated by the development of the Japanese military operations, the creation of the "Manchukuo Government" and the recognition of that "Government" by Japan. Undoubtedly the present case is not that of a country which has declared war on another country without previously exhausting the opportunities for conciliation provided in the Covenant of the League of Nations; neither is it a simple case of the violation of the frontier of one country by the armed forces of a neighbouring country, because in Manchuria, as shown by the circumstances noted above, there are many features without an exact parallel in other parts of the world. It is, however, indisputable that, without any declaration of war, a large part of Chinese territory has been forcibly seized and occupied by Japanese troops and that, in consequence of this operation, it has been separated from and declared independent of the rest of China.

(Bettmann/Corbis)

DEFINING MOMENT II

Roosevelt at the Yalta Conference

Introduction 76

Classroom Activities 78

Primary and Secondary Sources 96

Background Material 121

DEFINING MOMENT II

Introduction

The Yalta Conference was a defining moment that helped shape the postwar world. U.S. president Franklin D. Roosevelt, British prime minister Winston Churchill, and Soviet premier Joseph Stalin met during February 4–11, 1945, in the city of Yalta on the Crimean Peninsula to discuss the final stages of World War II. Unresolved issues between the "Big Three," as those leaders were known, were also discussed. Of noted importance were the fate of postwar Germany, the nature of postwar governments in Eastern Europe, and the establishment of a world organization to maintain the postwar peace.

Roosevelt's bargaining position at Yalta was a difficult one. Stalin possessed the largest army in Europe, and his forces had already occupied the bulk of Eastern Europe. With the possibility of a costly invasion of Japan looming for the United States, Roosevelt thought that securing Soviet participation in the final defeat of Japan was crucial. As a result, Roosevelt considered it necessary to make concessions in his negotiations with Stalin in order to secure agreements on the issues that he deemed most important.

The preeminent issue at the conference was the fate of postwar Germany. The Big Three agreed to divide Germany into four occupation zones (Roosevelt and Churchill convinced Stalin to allow France a zone), demilitarize Germany, and put German war criminals on trial. In addition, Roosevelt and Churchill acquiesced to Stalin's demand that Germany pay war reparations to compensate for the massive material damage and horrendous loss of life endured by the Soviet Union during the war.

In negotiating the fate of Eastern Europe, Roosevelt made a major concession on the issue of Poland. Roosevelt and Churchill recognized the legitimacy of the Polish government-in-exile in London, while Stalin conversely recognized a communist government that had been established in Lublin. Roosevelt was willing to shift his recognition to the Lublin government at Stalin's demand—based on the assumption that democratic elections would eventually be held to allow non-communist participation—in order to secure Soviet cooperation in other matters.

INTRODUCTION Roosevelt at the Yalta Conference

It was similarly agreed that interim governments would be established by the Soviets throughout Eastern Europe pending democratic elections. Because Eastern Europe was solely under Soviet occupation there was no way of ensuring that agreement, and Stalin subsequently reneged on his promise to allow free elections by establishing exclusively communist governments that directly answered to the authority of the Soviet leaders in Moscow.

A major goal for Roosevelt at the conference was achieving a specific commitment of Soviet assistance in the defeat of Japan. By secretly agreeing to the Soviet acquisition of territories in the Far East, Roosevelt secured Stalin's promise that he would declare war on Japan no later than ninety days after Germany's unconditional surrender. The Soviet Union did so on August 8, 1945, two days after the United States dropped an atomic bomb on the Japanese city of Hiroshima.

Roosevelt also considered the establishment of a world organization to be crucial. A draft proposal for the United Nations (UN) had already been created the previous year, but several matters remained to be negotiated. By agreeing to many of Stalin's demands, Roosevelt was able to convince him to participate in the UN while abandoning his demand that each of the sixteen Soviet republics have representation in the General Assembly, a proposal that was unacceptable to Churchill and Roosevelt.

By compromising with Stalin at Yalta, Roosevelt was able to secure agreements on the issues that he considered most important. His concessions on Eastern Europe, however, allowed for the spread of communism and thus contributed to the rise of the Cold War. While supporters felt that Roosevelt employed pragmatism at Yalta to achieve the best possible results, many critics felt that his achievements were overshadowed by what they considered a surrender of Eastern Europe.

CLASSROOM ACTIVITIES

Roosevelt at the Yalta Conference

AUTHOR

Chris Mullin
*Santa Ynez Valley
Union High School*

AUTHOR

Brett Piersma
*Santa Ynez Valley
Union High School*

This series of lessons will focus primarily on World War II and the Yalta Conference and will take place in two stages. The lessons will help students understand the issues surrounding President Roosevelt's compromises at the Yalta Conference.

Lesson 1 This lesson is designed to provide context for the Crimean (Yalta) Conference in February 1945. Students will learn the contrast between Western and Soviet goals for the postwar era as early as the beginning of the war.

Lesson 2 Through a role-playing exercise, students will recreate negotiations between Stalin, Churchill, and Roosevelt at the Yalta Conference.

CLASSROOM ACTIVITIES Roosevelt at the Yalta Conference

Lesson 1
Class Discussion

MATERIALS NEEDED

For this portion of the lesson, students will need

EXCERPTS OF DOCUMENTS
- A: Franklin Delano Roosevelt, Message to Congress, January 6, 1941, p. 97
- B: Excerpt from the Atlantic Charter, 1941, pp. 98–99
- C: Excerpt from the Declaration of the United Nations, 1942, p. 100
- D: Excerpt from the Secret Additional Protocol of the USSR, August 1939, p. 101

MAPS
- World War II, Map 1, p. 102
- World War II, Map 2, p. 103

First, for students to adequately understand what took place at Yalta, they will study the contrast between Western and Soviet goals for the postwar era as early as the beginning of the war.

The teacher should pass out to each student copies of the first three documents: excerpts from Franklin D. Roosevelt's speech to Congress, the Atlantic Charter, and the Declaration of the United Nations. The teacher should choose several students to read the documents to the class—about two or three students per document. The excerpts are short enough for students to digest the material in one quick read. The teacher should pose the following questions to the whole class and respond to students' questions regarding the goals of the Western nations:

- When were these documents written?
- Generally, what are the goals of the Western nations with regard to Europe after the war?
- Do you think these are reasonable and attainable goals? Why or why not?

Next the teacher should distribute copies of the excerpt from the Secret Additional Protocol of the USSR and the two maps. The teacher should ask several other students to read the document aloud, then draw students' attention to the maps. The teacher should ask the students to turn to a partner or form a group to discuss the following questions:

- What does the Secret Additional Protocol of the USSR indicate about the goals of the Soviet Union?
- Does the fact that the Soviets and the Nazis turned against one another change the Soviet's goals?
- Looking at the maps, what do you think the location of the Soviet Army means for the fate of Poland? Is there a possibility that Poland will see "free and democratic" elections in the postwar era? Why or why not?

At this point students should have a solid understanding of the disparate goals of the West and the Soviet Union. The teacher may assess students' grasp of these concepts with a ten-minute Quickwrite or essay prompt in which students must compare the goals of the two sides and weigh the validity of each.

CLASSROOM ACTIVITIES Roosevelt at the Yalta Conference

Lesson 2
Role Playing

MATERIALS NEEDED

For this portion of the lesson, students will need

HANDOUTS
- Ten Role Cards, pp. 83–92
- Worksheet A: Protocol of Proceedings of the Crimea Conference, February 1945, pp. 93–94
- Worksheet B: Newspaper Article Storyboard, p. 95

PHOTOGRAPHS
- Image A: Stalin and Churchill, p. 104
- Image B: Yalta Conference: Churchill, Roosevelt, and Stalin, p. 105
- Image C: Yalta Conference Roundtable, p. 106
- Image D: A Crimean Huddle, p. 107

POLITICAL CARTOONS
- Image E: *Hoover Digest* cartoon, p. 108
- Image F: "Fifty-fifty Again, Joe?," p. 109
- Image G: "The Repairman," p. 110

NEWSPAPER ARTICLES
- Image H: *The New York Times:* Nazism and Reich Militarism, p. 111
- Document E: Translation of Stalin's Message to the Nation, pp. 112–113

EXCERPTS OF DOCUMENTS
- Document F: Protocol of Proceedings of Crimea Conference, February 1945, pp. 114–115
- Document G: Protocol of Proceedings of Crimea Conference, February 1945, pp. 116–117
- Document H: Protocol of Proceedings of Crimea Conference, February 1945, pp. 118–119
- Document I: Protocol of Proceedings of Crimea Conference, February 1945, p. 120

Using the Yalta agreement, images, and maps of Europe, student groups will recreate the negotiations between Stalin, Churchill, and Roosevelt at the Yalta Conference.

First, the teacher should ask the following questions to guide students in understanding what was at stake during the Yalta conference and who had the upper ground:

- Which country's army had a stronger presence in Europe early in 1945?
- How would this advantage benefit that country during the conference?

Next, the teacher should divide students into groups of ten and have each group form a large circle. Each student within a group should be given one of the following roles and a copy of the related document, in parentheses in the list on the next page (if smaller groups are needed, the three journalist roles can be deleted).

CLASSROOM ACTIVITIES Roosevelt at the Yalta Conference

1. United States president Franklin D. Roosevelt (Document G)
2. Harry Hopkins, advisor to Mr. Roosevelt (Document G)
3. British prime minister Winston Churchill (Document H)
4. Sir Edward Ian Jacob, advisor to Mr. Churchill (Document H)
5. Russian premier Joseph Stalin (Document I)
6. Deputy foreign commissar Ivan Maysky, advisor to Mr. Stalin (Document I)
7. American journalist (Images A–H)
8. British journalist (Images A–F, H)
9. Soviet journalist (Images A–D, Document E)
10. Moderator (Document F)

The teacher should tell each student group that they will be simulating the Yalta Conference and should base all of their decisions on what they have learned about the goals of each side in addition to the political and military realities in Europe in early 1945.

To get started, the teacher should provide each student with his or her role card and related documents that outline the student's role at the Yalta Conference. Each delegation (leaders and advisors) and the moderator will be given a different portion of the actual Protocol that was agreed upon at Yalta to guide their negotiations. This is provided to make sure each group creates an end product that somewhat resembles the actual text of the Yalta agreement. Students should read this document before the negotiations begin and keep this document secret from the other delegations.

Next, the teacher should provide the moderator of each group with Worksheet A, Protocol of Proceedings of the Crimea Conference, February 1945, and tell them to follow the instructions on the role card to complete it during the conference.

For each journalist, the teacher should provide Worksheet B, Newspaper Article Storyboard and the documents listed above for them to base their articles and images on. The teacher should instruct them that their task is to report back to their newspapers on what they witnessed. Journalists should use the worksheet to plan everything in their article from the headline to the images they will use; they should use the provided documents and images as a guide. Their work, however, should be unique and should not be a copy of the documents they used. Additionally, each article should reflect a bias in favor of the journalist's own country, but should not blatantly distort facts or events.

Before conducting the conferences, the teacher should give students about five or ten minutes to read their role cards and documents and to plan their approach.

Continues on next page

CLASSROOM ACTIVITIES Roosevelt at the Yalta Conference

Lesson 2, continued

The next step is to begin the conferences. The teacher should move between the groups to make sure they are on the right track and that students are playing their roles appropriately. The teacher may wish to include an incentive for the delegation from each group that achieves the most favorable agreement. Once the groups have decided on each issue and signed their documents, the teacher should collect their agreements and pull the class together, then debrief with the following questions:

- Which delegation was the most difficult to work with?
- Which delegation achieved the most favorable agreement? Do you think that accurately reflects what took place at the Yalta Conference? Why or why not?
- What was difficult about negotiating? What was easy?
- If you were actually at the Yalta Conference, how would you have dealt with the variety of personalities in attendance?

After the conferences, the teacher may assign the following tasks to assess students' involvement and how thoroughly they grasped the big concepts at issue at Yalta:

Moderator—Each moderator should prepare a one-page "Statement to the Press" to be published in all newspapers in all countries. It should reflect a neutral and unbiased perspective on the proceedings at Yalta and should be addressed "To the International Community."

Leader—Each leader should write a one-page speech to be given to the citizens of their country summarizing what took place at Yalta and how it benefits their country and people.

Advisor—Each advisor should write a one-page journal entry for the purposes of his or her memoir summarizing the advisor's thoughts about the events at Yalta.

Journalists—Using their storyboard, each journalist should write a one-page article to be submitted to their editors for publication. They should include their cartoon(s) or drawing(s).

CLASSROOM ACTIVITIES Roosevelt at the Yalta Conference

Lesson 2
Role Card

Role
United States President Franklin D. Roosevelt

Related Document
Document G, pp. 116–117

Description of Role
You will be portraying President Roosevelt at the Yalta Conference simulation. The goals you wish to achieve at the conference are (1) to create a "united nations" to settle international disputes in the postwar era and to secure the participation of the Soviets in the new organization; (2) to draw Stalin into the war against Japan in order to hasten the defeat of Japan; and (3) to foster a spirit of trust and cooperation between the United States and the Soviet Union. Work with your advisor to decide the issues for which you will fight and the issues on which you will negotiate.

How to Portray the Role
Having been crippled by polio at a young age, you are mostly confined to a wheelchair and are currently not well. You have just made the long trip from the United States to Crimea (on the Black Sea) and are exhausted. Within several months of the conference you will be dead. As you portray the president, keep his condition in mind. He is idealistic and has grand goals but is perhaps less aggressive than he once was. Fight for your goals, but be willing to compromise in order to keep the conference moving forward. Act tired and worn-out, yet focused and determined.

CLASSROOM ACTIVITIES Roosevelt at the Yalta Conference

Lesson 2
Role Card

Role
Harry Hopkins, Advisor to Mr. Roosevelt

Related Document
Document G, pp. 116–117

Description of Role
You will be portraying Harry Hopkins, a long-time friend and advisor to President Roosevelt. Your job is to help the president remain tough in the face of demands for concessions by the Soviets and to keep his focus on his goals. Help him decide the issues for which he should fight and the issues on which he should negotiate.

How to Portray the Role
As a long-time friend and confidant you can speak candidly to the president and be forceful. However, make sure you allow the president to make the final decision on each issue brought to the table. Additionally, you are suffering from an illness that leaves you weak. At the end of the conference you will be exhausted and feel frustrated by the outcome and the decisions. You and the president will part ways on a sour note and will never see one another again.

CLASSROOM ACTIVITIES Roosevelt at the Yalta Conference

Lesson 2
Role Card

Role
British Prime Minister Winston Churchill

Related Document
Document H, pp. 118–119

Description of Role
You will be portraying the British prime minister, Winston Churchill. Your primary goals at the conference are (1) to ensure free, democratic elections in Eastern Europe; (2) to secure the liberation of Poland after the defeat of Nazi Germany; and (3) to ensure that Germany NOT be forced to make payment of reparations after the war. Work with your advisor to decide the issues for which you will fight and the issues on which you will negotiate.

How to Portray the Role
As the fearless leader of Britain during the war, you are battle-hardened and bold, and very fond of cigars. You have withstood the onslaught of the German Luftwaffe during the Battle of Britain and have seen dark times for your country. Now, as the defeat of the Nazis is imminent, you are highly confident in your leadership and vision. As you and Mr. Roosevelt have developed a firm friendship during the war, you frequently will lean over to him to discuss a point in private before making a statement to the whole group. Use your leadership skills to secure the best terms for your country at the conference.

Lesson 2
Role Card

Role
Sir Edward Ian Jacob, Advisor to Mr. Churchill

Related Document
Document H, pp. 118–119

Description of Role
As an advisor to Mr. Churchill at the Yalta Conference, your job is to ensure that the prime minister sticks to his guns and secures the goals that are most important to your nation. Help him decide the issues for which he should fight and the issues on which he should negotiate.

How to Portray the Role
You have served in the War Cabinet for your country and have attended many of these war conferences. You know how to make tough decisions and how to deal with tough deal makers. While you don't want to dominate the discussion at the conference table, make sure you are a calm, rational voice and ally for Churchill. Ultimately, make sure you allow Mr. Churchill to make the final decisions on whatever is discussed at the table.

CLASSROOM ACTIVITIES Roosevelt at the Yalta Conference

Lesson 2
Role Card

Role
Russian Premier Joseph Stalin

Related Document
Document I, p. 120

Description of Role
You are playing the bombastic and arrogant Russian premier Joseph Stalin. At the time of the conference, your army occupies most of Eastern Europe and is poised to make the final strike against Hitler to cause his defeat. You have several important goals for the conference: (1) to ensure the creation of a Soviet "sphere of influence" in Eastern Europe that will serve as a buffer against Germany into the future; (2) to secure permanent membership on the powerful United Nations Security Council and veto power of any decisions; (3) to gain additional territory in the form of islands controlled by Japan such as Sakhalin and the Kuril islands. Work with your advisor to decide the issues for which you will fight and issues on which you will negotiate.

How to Portray the Role
Very early in the conference, you must persuade the other members of the conference that you are NOT negotiable on the question of Poland. Be passionate and convince them that Poland is vital to the security of your country as a buffer zone. You can consent to free elections there, but would have no intentions of actually allowing them to go forward (unless of course they are rigged). Be arrogant and control the discussion. Be hesitant to give in on points. Realize that with your Red Army currently occupying Eastern Europe all the way into Germany with three times as many troops as the United States' army, you are in an extremely strong position to negotiate. Do not hesitate to mention this fact and use it against the other delegations.

CLASSROOM ACTIVITIES Roosevelt at the Yalta Conference

Lesson 2
Role Card

Role
Ivan Maysky, Advisor to Mr. Stalin

Related Document
Document I, p. 120

Description of Role
You will be portraying the deputy foreign commissar, Ivan Maysky, an important advisor to Mr. Stalin. While you are an accomplished Russian diplomat and ambassador, your primary role here is to agree with Stalin. You should not correct or interrupt him during the conference.

How to Portray the Role
Throughout the meeting you should frequently make approving nods whenever Stalin is speaking. When you speak, you should reiterate and confirm what Stalin has already said or praise him to the group for his fearless leadership and fair negotiating. Doing this will gain for you Stalin's favor, which is your tool for political advancement.

CLASSROOM ACTIVITIES Roosevelt at the Yalta Conference

Lesson 2
Role Card

Role
American Journalist

Related Documents
Images A–H, pp. 104–111

Description of Role
You will be portraying an American journalist working for *The New York Times* attending the conference at Yalta. Your job is to obtain quotes from each of the delegates as they discuss important topics at the conference and write a Newspaper Article Storyboard summarizing the conference. You want to write a high-quality story for your newspaper in order to advance your own career. However, as in all times of war, your patriotism may lead you to make Mr. Roosevelt seem more aggressive and firm than he really is. Additionally, your article must include a political cartoon or a drawing depicting the conference. Use the samples as a guide.

How to Portray the Role
Technically, you would not have been allowed to sit at the table during this historic conference. So during this simulation, you should sit quietly and take notes. Follow the discussions and arguments closely so you can get word-for-word quotes and write an accurate article on the conference afterward.

Lesson 2
Role Card

Role
British Journalist

Related Documents
Images A–F and H, pp. 104–109, p. 111

Description of Role
You will be portraying a British journalist working for the *Manchester Guardian* attending the conference at Yalta. Your job is to obtain quotes from each of the delegates as they discuss important topics at the conference and write a Newspaper Article Storyboard summarizing the conference. You not only want to write a high-quality story for your newspaper, but you also want to make your country's leader appear better than the others. Additionally, your article must include a political cartoon or a drawing depicting the conference. Use the samples as a guide.

How to Portray the Role
Technically, you would not have been allowed to sit at the table during this historic conference. So during this simulation, you should sit quietly and take notes. Follow the discussions and arguments closely so you can get word-for-word quotes and write an accurate article on the conference afterward.

CLASSROOM ACTIVITIES Roosevelt at the Yalta Conference

Lesson 2
Role Card

Role
Soviet Journalist

Related Documents
Images A–D and Document E, pp. 104–107, pp. 112–113

Description of Role
You will be portraying a journalist working for the *Pravda* newspaper in Russia. Being a communist country, the Soviet Union controls the content of newspapers, which does not give you much choice in how to write your article. You must write an article that glorifies Stalin and you can even twist and distort the truth with misquotes in order to make him appear superior to the other leaders. Doing this is a matter of life and death for you as a journalist because you work directly for the government, and the government relies on you for much of its propaganda. Writing that is critical of the government or Premier Stalin would be punished by imprisonment in the Gulag or death. Your article must include a political cartoon or a drawing depicting the conference, but be careful not to criticize Papa Stalin!

How to Portray the Role
Technically, you would not have been allowed to sit at the table during this historic conference. So during this simulation, you should sit quietly and take notes. Follow the discussions and arguments closely so you can get quotes and ideas for what to write. Remember, your article will be used as propaganda by the State to further its own agenda.

CLASSROOM ACTIVITIES Roosevelt at the Yalta Conference

Lesson 2
Role Card

Role
Moderator

Related Document
Document F, pp. 114–115

Description of Role
You will be the moderator and writer at the Yalta Conference. Your job is to ensure that the group comes to an agreement on each of the topics on the agenda. Additionally, you will facilitate the discussion and make sure that all members are allowed to speak and make their points heard. Once a decision has been reached on an issue, you must fill in the corresponding blanks on Worksheet A—Protocol of Proceedings of the Crimea Conference. Once all sides are agreeable to the final set of agreements, have each leader sign the bottom of the document and turn it in to the teacher.

How to Portray the Role
As the moderator, make sure you are diplomatic in your approach to disagreements. Give all sides a chance to air their grievances and work with each to come to a resolution. You may have to encourage one side to give in on an issue by promising them that another issue will be decided in their favor. Above all, keep the group working together and moving.

CLASSROOM ACTIVITIES Roosevelt at the Yalta Conference

Lesson 2
Worksheet A, Side 1

Protocol of Proceedings of the Crimea Conference, February 1945

The Crimea Conference of the heads of the Governments of the United States of America, the United Kingdom, and the Union of Soviet Socialist Republics, which took place from February 4 to 11, came to the following conclusions:

I. WORLD ORGANIZATION

It was decided:

1.

2.

3.

II. DECLARATION OF LIBERATED EUROPE

With regard to the common interests of the people of their countries and those of liberated Europe the following decisions have been approved:

1.

2.

3.

(See next page for Side 2)

Lesson 2
Worksheet A, Side 2

III. AGREEMENT REGARDING JAPAN

With regard to the Empire of Japan, the leaders of the three great powers—the Soviet Union, the United States of America, and Great Britain—have agreed that

1.

2.

3.

IV. AGREEMENT REGARDING POLAND

The following declaration on Poland was agreed by the conference:

1.

2.

3.

Signed: _____

CLASSROOM ACTIVITIES Roosevelt at the Yalta Conference

DEFINING MOMENT II

Lesson 2
Worksheet B

Newspaper Article Storyboard

Article Title: _____

Article Subtitle: _____

Descriptions of three images to include in the article:

Three quotes from the conference you will incorporate into the article:

Three other facts you will include in the article:

On the back, draw a political cartoon or picture depicting one event from the conference.

95

PRIMARY AND SECONDARY SOURCES

Roosevelt at the Yalta Conference

SOURCES Roosevelt at the Yalta Conference

Lesson 1 Document
Document A

Franklin Delano Roosevelt, Message to Congress, January 6, 1941

We look forward to a world founded upon four essential human freedoms. The first is freedom of speech and expression—everywhere in the world. The second is freedom of every person to worship God in his own way—everywhere in the world. The third is freedom from want . . . everywhere in the world. The fourth is freedom from fear . . . anywhere in the world.

Lesson 1 Document
Document B

Excerpt from the Atlantic Charter, 1941

In July 1941, Franklin D. Roosevelt and Winston Churchill met off Newfoundland to issue a declaration on the purposes of the war. The Soviet Union was intended to sign the charter as well, but Joseph Stalin rejected the concept of "one world," in which nations banded together militarily. Roosevelt, however, truly believed in the possibility of a world governed by democratic processes, with an international organization serving as an arbiter of disputes and protector of the peace.

The President of the United States of America and the Prime Minister, Mr. Churchill, representing His Majesty's Government in the United Kingdom, being met together, deem it right to make known certain common principles in the national policies of their respective countries on which they base their hopes for a better future for the world.

First, their countries seek no aggrandizement, territorial or other;

Second, they desire to see no territorial changes that do not accord with the freely expressed wishes of the peoples concerned;

Third, they respect the right of all peoples to choose the form of government under which they will live; and they wish to see sovereign rights and self government restored to those who have been forcibly deprived of them;

. . .

SOURCES Roosevelt at the Yalta Conference

Lesson 1 Document
Document B, continued

Sixth, after the final destruction of the Nazi tyranny, they hope to see established a peace which will afford to all nations the means of dwelling in safety within their own boundaries, and which will afford assurance that all the men in all the lands may live out their lives in freedom from fear and want;

. . .

Eighth, they believe that all of the nations of the world, for realistic as well as spiritual reasons must come to the abandonment of the use of force. Since no future peace can be maintained if land, sea or air armaments continue to be employed by nations which threaten, or may threaten, aggression outside of their frontiers, they believe, pending the establishment of a wider and permanent system of general security, that the disarmament of such nations is essential. They will likewise aid and encourage all other practicable measures which will lighten for peace-loving peoples the crushing burden of armaments.

Franklin D. Roosevelt
Winston S. Churchill

Lesson 1 Document
Document C

Excerpt from the Declaration of the United Nations, 1942

A Joint Declaration by the United States, the United Kingdom, the Union of Soviet Socialist Republics, China, Australia, Belgium, Canada, Costa Rica, Cuba, Czechoslovakia, Dominican Republic, El Salvador, Greece, Guatemala, Haiti, Honduras, India, Luxembourg, Netherlands, New Zealand, Nicaragua, Norway, Panama, Poland, South Africa, Yugoslavia

The Governments signatory hereto,

Having subscribed to a common program of purposes and principles embodied in the Joint Declaration of the President of the United States of America and the Prime Minister of the United Kingdom of Great Britain and Northern Ireland dated August 14, 1941, known as the Atlantic Charter.

Being convinced that complete victory over their enemies is essential to defend life, liberty, independence and religious freedom, and to preserve human rights and justice in their own lands as well as in other lands, and that they are now engaged in a common struggle against savage and brutal forces seeking to subjugate the world,

DECLARE:

(1) Each Government pledges itself to employ its full resources, military or economic, against those members of the Tripartite Pact and its adherents with which such government is at war.

(2) Each Government pledges itself to cooperate with the Governments signatory hereto and not to make a separate armistice or peace with the enemies.

The foregoing declaration may be adhered to by other nations which are, or which may be, rendering material assistance and contributions in the struggle for victory over Hitlerism.

Done at Washington
January First, 1942

SOURCES Roosevelt at the Yalta Conference

Lesson 1 Document
Document D

Excerpt from the Secret Additional Protocol of the USSR, August 1939

On the occasion of the signature of the Nonaggression Pact between the German Reich and the Union of Socialist Soviet Republics the undersigned plenipotentiaries of each of the two parties discussed in strictly confidential conversations the question of the boundary of their respective spheres of influence in Eastern Europe. These conversations led to the following conclusions:

1. In the event of a territorial and political rearrangement in the areas belonging to the Baltic States (Finland, Estonia, Latvia, Lithuania), the northern boundary of Lithuania shall represent the boundary of the spheres of influence of Germany and the U.S.S.R. In this connection the interest of Lithuania in the Vilna area is recognized by each party.

2. In the event of a territorial and political rearrangement of the areas belonging to the Polish state the spheres of influence of Germany and the U.S.S.R. shall be bounded approximately by the line of the rivers Narew, Vistula, and San.

The question of whether the interests of both parties make desirable the maintenance of an independent Polish state and how such a state should be bounded can only be definitely determined in the course of further political developments.

In any event both Governments will resolve this question by means of a friendly agreement.

3. With regard to Southeastern Europe attention is called by the Soviet side to its interest in Bessarabia. The German side declares its complete political disinterestedness in these areas.

This protocol shall be treated by both parties as strictly secret.

Moscow, August 23, 1939.

For the Government of the German Reich:

V. RIBBENTROP

Plenipotentiary of the Government of the U.S.S.R.:

V. MOLOTOV

SOURCES Roosevelt at the Yalta Conference

Lesson 1 Map
World War II, Map 1

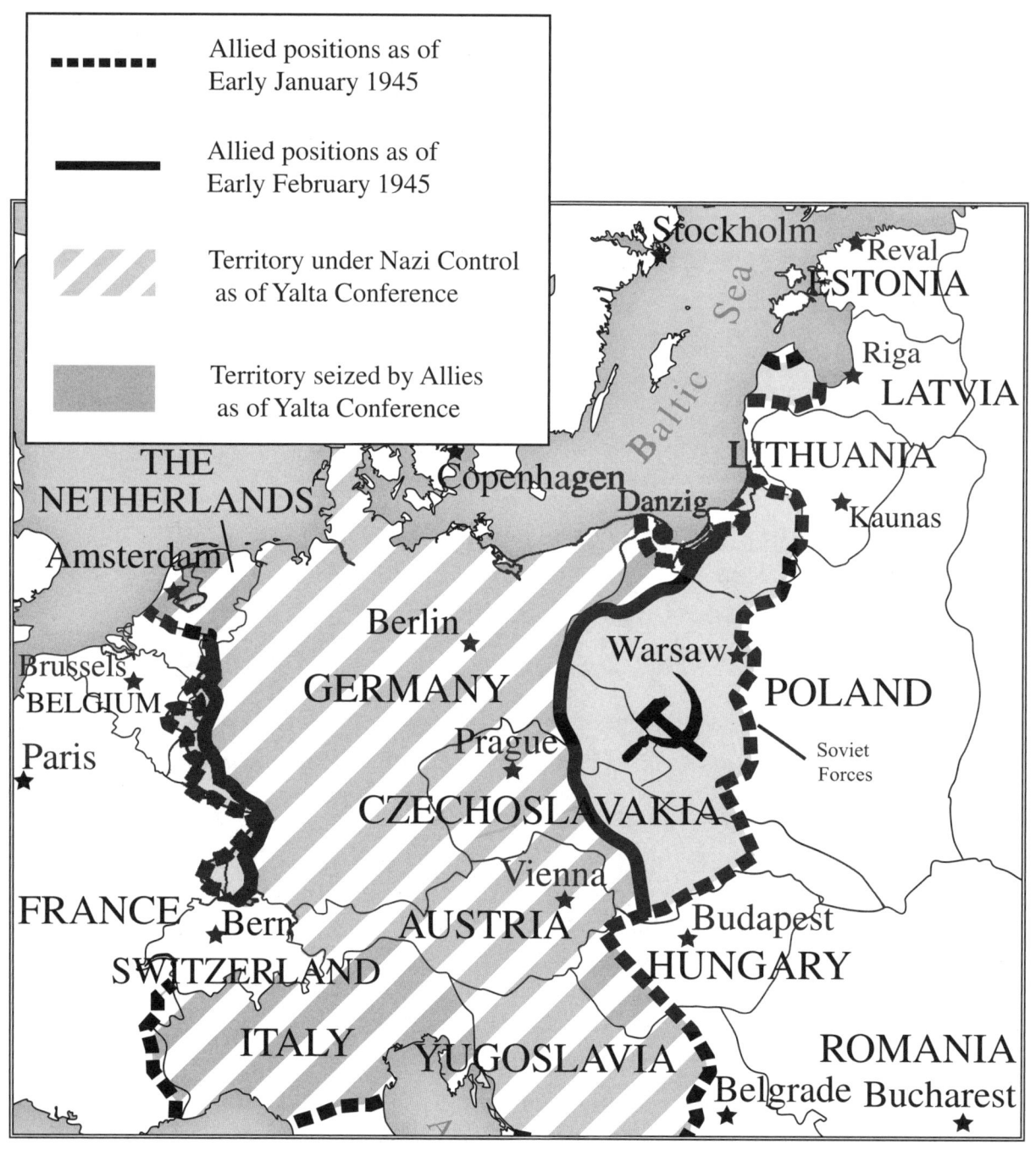

SOURCES Roosevelt at the Yalta Conference

Lesson 1 Map
World War II, Map 2

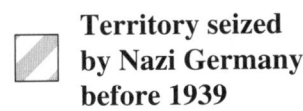
Territory seized by Nazi Germany before 1939

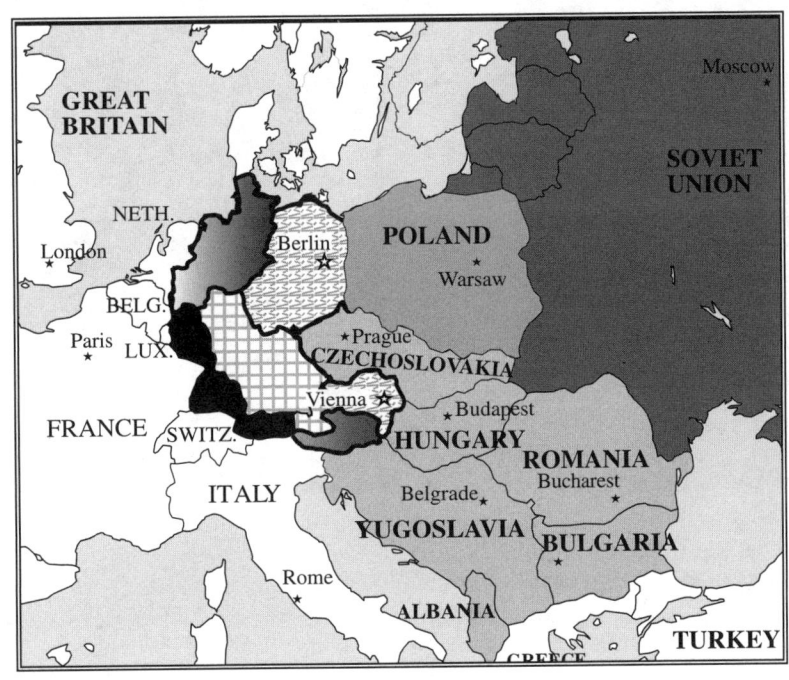

- Soviet Union
- Soviet Satellites
- Soviet Occupation Zone
- French Occupation Zone
- British Occupation Zone
- U.S. Occupation Zone
- Poland (Soviet Satellite)

SOURCES Roosevelt at the Yalta Conference

Lesson 2 Photograph
Image A
Stalin and Churchill

▲ This photograph of Winston Churchill and Joseph Stalin, taken at the Yalta Conference in 1945, belies the deep mistrust between the two leaders. (Library of Congress)

SOURCES Roosevelt at the Yalta Conference

Lesson 2 Photograph
Image B
Yalta Conference: Churchill, Roosevelt, and Stalin

▲ British prime minister Winston Churchill (left), U.S. president Franklin D. Roosevelt (center), and Soviet leader Josef Stalin (right) at the Yalta Conference. The "Big Three" met in Yalta, Crimea (in what is now the Ukraine) on February 4–11, 1945, to discuss military and political strategy. (Library of Congress)

SOURCES Roosevelt at the Yalta Conference

Lesson 2 Photograph
Image C
Yalta Conference Roundtable

▲ Winston Churchill (far right), Joseph Stalin (far left) and Franklin Roosevelt (center) sit around the conference table at the Yalta Conference near the end of World War II. Also present are Andrei Gromyko (to Stalin's left), Admiral William Leahy (beside Gromyko), Edward Stettinius (beside Leahy), and James Byrnes (one man right of FDR). (Bettmann/Corbis)

SOURCES Roosevelt at the Yalta Conference

Lesson 2 Photograph
Image D
A Crimean Huddle

▲ An ailing Franklin D. Roosevelt shows the strain of overwork as he huddles with Winston Churchill in the Banquet Room of Livadia Palace, Yalta, 1945. (Library of Congress)

DEFINING MOMENT II

SOURCES Roosevelt at the Yalta Conference

Lesson 2 Cartoon
Image E
Hoover Digest Cartoon

▲ This modern satirical political cartoon depicts a triumphant Franklin D. Roosevelt along with Winston Churchill and Joseph Stalin. (© 2004 Taylor Jones. Courtesy of *Hoover Digest*)

SOURCES Roosevelt at the Yalta Conference

Lesson 2 Cartoon
Image F
"Fifty-fifty Again, Joe?"

DEFINING MOMENT II

▲ Adolf Hitler and Joseph Stalin had previously agreed on the division of Eastern Europe and might have contemplated this division of Iraq and Iran. Instead, Hitler invaded the Soviet Union on June 22, 1941. (The Herb Block Foundation)

SOURCES Roosevelt at the Yalta Conference

Lesson 2 Cartoon
Image G
"The Repairman"

▲ This cartoon by artist Edwin Marcus depicts the task of the "Big 4" as repairing a broken Europe, Asia, and Africa at the end of the war, circa 1945. (Library of Congress)

Lesson 2 Newspaper Article

Image H
The New York Times: Nazism and Reich Militarism

"All the News That's Fit to Print"

The New York Times.

LATE CITY EDITION
Increasing cloudiness with moderate winds today.
Temperatures Yesterday—Max., 46; Min., 29
Sunrise today, 7:55 A. M.; Sunset, 6:16 P. M.

Copyright, 1945, by The New York Times Company.

VOL. XCIV...No. 31,797. Entered as Second-Class Matter, Postoffice, New York, N. Y. NEW YORK, TUESDAY, FEBRUARY 13, 1945. THREE CENTS NEW YORK CITY

BIG 3 DOOM NAZISM AND REICH MILITARISM; AGREE ON FREED LANDS AND OAKS VOTING; CONVOKE UNITED NATIONS IN U. S. APRIL 25

IVES ASSAILS FOES OF ANTI-RACE BILLS AS DISFAVOR RISES

But Demand for Immediate Vote by CIO Head Is Unlikely to Head Off Opposition

PRESS FOR PUBLIC HEARING

Legislators Confident of Aid From Minorities—Chamber Attack Called 'Degrading'

The text of the statement by Assemblyman Ives, Page 18.

Special to THE NEW YORK TIMES.

ALBANY, Feb. 12—Irving M. Ives, Republican leader of the Assembly, and Louis Hollander, president of the State Congress of Industrial Organizations, struck back tonight at critics of the Ives-Quinn anti-discrimination bills.

In a statement defending the proposal to set up a five-man commission with power to eradicate discrimination in employment on racial or religious grounds, Mr. Ives sought to set at rest a strong feeling that it would have the effect of increasing rather than eliminating interracial frictions.

Meanwhile, opposition to the measure continued to grow. It was believed that neither Mr. Ives' statement nor Mr. Hollander's appeal to pass the Ives-Quinn proposals "at once and without any crippling amendments" appear likely to head off that opposition.

Pressure for Public Hearing

In the Senate, where the bill remains in the Finance Committee, there is very strong pressure for a public hearing. Senator Elmer F. Quinn, Democratic leader of the Senate and co-sponsor with Mr. Ives of the legislation, described the pressure for a hearing as "terrific."

Mr. Quinn said that he had been besieged in New York over the week-end by representatives of employment agencies who want an opportunity to present amendments to the bill. But supporters of the measure are opposed to granting further hearings.

Advocates of the legislation also believe that only a few legislators will dare to vote against the measure in view of the strong demand for its passage from CIO unions, Negro and other minority groups.

Some Republican strategists are viewing the proposal as an opportunity to regain the favor of minority groups. Democratic leaders in turn are cracking the whip to obtain a solid Democratic vote in favor of the legislation in both Senate and Assembly.

Governor Dewey has avoided taking any stand on the measure, but he has gone on record in his annual message in favor of the enactment of bills along the lines of the Ives-Quinn proposal to put "our

WPB Takes Charge Of Match Output

By The Associated Press.

WASHINGTON, Feb. 12—The War Production Board took control today over production and distribution of matches, to assure, it said, the meeting of military requirements and preventing maldistribution of civilian supplies.

The allocation of matches will be controlled at the producer level.

Production of matches this year is expected to total 460,000,000,000 as compared with an average pre-war level of 480,000,000,000. The reduced production is attributed to the labor shortage.

Military requirements will take about a third of the 1945 output, including the entire production of strike-on-box matches and about 35 per cent of the book matches.

Civilians will find it more difficult to obtain strike-on-box and book matches, but the WPB said that the supply of strike-anywhere, or kitchen, matches would be adequate if there were no hoarding.

BIG 3 AGREEMENT LAUDED BY HOOVER

'Strong Foundation' for New World, He Says—Austin Asks Bipartisan Planning

Before 1,000 persons high in the leadership of the Republican party, former President Herbert Hoover, long a spokesman for an important section of his party, gave an enthusiastic endorsement last night to the agreement reached by President Roosevelt, Marshal Joseph Stalin and Prime Minister Winston Churchill at the Big Three conference in the Crimea.

Called upon for an impromptu speech at the fifty-ninth annual Lincoln Day dinner of the National Republican Club at the Hotel Waldorf-Astoria, Mr. Hoover said he believed the agreement provided "a strong foundation" for the reconstruction of the post-war world. He said:

"On the radio this evening there was announced news of tremendous importance to the whole world. That is the agreement reached in the Black Sea area.

"I believe it comprises a strong foundation on which to rebuild the world.

"If the agreement's promises and ideals which are expressed shall be carried out, it will open a great hope to the world.

"It is fitting that it should have been issued to the world on the birthday of Abraham Lincoln."

As Mr. Hoover resumed his seat after his brief remarks, there was applause from every section of the audience.

Senator Warren R. Austin of Vermont, another speaker at the gathering, joined Mr. Hoover in

CLEVE, PRUEM FALL

Allies Capture Two Key Westwall Positions in North and Center

OPPOSITION IS LIGHT

Germans Draft Women for Volkssturm—New Clashes Reported

By CLIFTON DANIEL
By Wireless to THE NEW YORK TIMES.

SUPREME HEADQUARTERS, Allied Expeditionary Force, Feb. 12—With surprising dispatch, Allied troops broke the Germans' hold on key centers of two sectors of the Western Front today, evicting all except a few snipers from Cleve, at the northern end of the line, and from Pruem, in the center.

British and Canadian forces quickly mopped up the Siegfried fortress town of Cleve and also pressed through the full length of the Reichswald (Reich Forest) to its eastern edge.

Gen. H. D. G. Crerar's forces also were converging on Goch, a German position southeast of the Reichswald comparable to that of Cleve in the north. One force had captured Hau, seven miles north of Goch, while another unit was at Kessel, four miles northwest.

[Due west of Goch, General Crerar's forces also cleared Gennep, another fortified town in that area, press services reported.]

Patton Sets Up New Threat

At the same time Lieut. Gen. George S. Patton's American Third Army fought to merge two of its bridgeheads across the Sauer River, twenty-five miles south of Pruem, into a solid six-mile front that would present a new threat to the road and rail network west of Bonn and Coblenz, of which Pruem was one important hub.

[As the two important Westwall strong points of Cleve and Pruem fell, Germany conscripted all women from 16 to 60 years of age for service in the Volkssturm, while reports from Sweden, Switzerland and Moscow told of mounting unrest and new clashes inside Germany, press services said.]

While the slow but ominous encroachments of the Allies' pent-up strength continued, the Germans were apparently hoping to flood out the Allies' armies, which they repeatedly have reported were ready to attack. A German communiqué today said the flooding of the Roer River Valley had forced the Allies to abandon positions in many sectors and to abandon preparations for an attack.

A natural flooding already made operations extremely difficult on the northern flank of the Canadian First Army's advance around

THE BIG THREE MEETING AGAIN TO MAKE PLANS FOR THE WORLD

Prime Minister Churchill, President Roosevelt and Marshal Stalin on the grounds of Livadia Palace
The New York Times (British Official Radiophoto)

MANILA TRAP SHUT; LUZON IS CROSSED

U. S. Forces Unite to Squeeze Capital as Armored Push East Reaches Coast

By GEORGE E. JONES
By Wireless to THE NEW YORK TIMES.

MANILA, Tuesday, Feb. 13—A broad front of American troops embracing three divisions now confronts the stubbornly resisting Japanese garrison in Manila, and there is reason to believe that the drive to complete seizure of the Orient's fourth largest city has now been accelerated.

The First Cavalry Division vet-

Continued on Page 16, Column 3

Red Army Is at Bober River After 16-Mile Gain in Silesia

By The United Press.

LONDON, Tuesday, Feb. 13—Red Army forces, opening the second month of their Winter offensive, pushed sixteen miles across Silesia yesterday in an outflanking drive southeast of Berlin that carried to within seventy-four miles of Dresden. Marshal Ivan S. Koneff's First Ukrainian Army seized 100 Silesian communities as it advanced westward from its bridgehead on the west bank of the Oder and reached the Bober River on a fifteen-mile front. Berlin said the Russians already had forced the Bober at two points.

Far behind the main fighting front, the Russians all but crushed the last organized resistance in long-besieged Budapest, having

Continued on Page 10, Column 5

War News Summarized

TUESDAY, FEBRUARY 13, 1945

"Nazi Germany is doomed . . . Only when nazism and militarism have been extirpated will there be hope for a decent life for Germans, and a place for them in the comity of nations."

That was the message for the "common enemy" emanating from Yalta, in the Crimea, where President Roosevelt, Prime Minister Churchill and Premier Stalin, completing their historic conference, made clear the meaning of "unconditional surrender."

The combined military plans call for even more powerful blows from all directions, said their report made public yester-

Yugoslavia was urged to put the Tito-Subasitch agreement into immediate effect and create a broad, provisional Parliament.

The Foreign Secretaries of the three nations will meet three or four times a year. The first time will be after a United Nations Conference to open in San Francisco April 25, which will prepare a charter along the lines of Dumbarton Oaks for the new international organization to maintain peace and security. [All the foregoing 1:8.]

While no mention was made of the Pacific war, it was pointed out that the period for denuncia-

PACIFIC WAR ROLE FOR SOVIET HINTED

Date of United Nations Parley Follows 'Denouncing' Time of Russo-Japanese Treaty

By JAMES B. RESTON
Special to THE NEW YORK TIMES.

WASHINGTON, Feb. 12—The positive announcements in the Crimean communiqué produced general satisfaction in Washington tonight, but what really interested the capital were the things the Big Three statement did not even mention.

The first of these was Japan. The word does not appear in the longest communiqué ever issued after a meeting of the heads of state, but the date set for the opening of the United Nations Security Conference in San Francisco, April 25, is the day after the date on which Russia must denounce her five-year neutrality pact with Japan unless she wishes it to run for another five years.

There is naturally some reticence here about any hasty conclusions in regard to so decisive a factor in

ROOSEVELT PRESSES WORLD MONEY PLAN

He Asks Congress for Action on Monetary Fund and on Bank of Reconstruction

The President's message on world monetary unity, Page 17.

Special to THE NEW YORK TIMES.

WASHINGTON, Feb. 12—President Roosevelt urged Congress today to take immediate action on the Bretton Woods proposals for an international monetary fund and an international bank for reconstruction and development.

In a special message, the President said that the two projects, involving legislation for American participation in the $8,800,000,000 stabilization fund and the $9,100,000,000 bank, were essential "in our plans for a peaceful and prosperous world," which, he said, could be attained "only if solutions are found to the difficult economic problems we face today."

Mr. Roosevelt recognized the criticisms directed against the stabilization fund proposal, mostly by United States banking groups, by conceding that it was not perfect, but suggested that experience would permit necessary improvements to be made.

Wagner Plans Bill

He asked Congress to act with special promptness on the plan for the international bank, which would guarantee loans for important development and reconstruction projects in the member countries. But

YALTA PARLEY ENDS

Unified Blows at Reich, Policing Spheres and Reparations Shaped

FRANCE TO GET ROLE

Broader Polish, Yugoslav Regimes Guaranteed—Curzon Line Adopted

The text of the report on the Big Three Conference, Page 4.

By LANSING WARREN
Special to THE NEW YORK TIMES.

WASHINGTON, Feb. 12—Allied decisions sealing the doom of Nazi Germany and German militarism, coordinating military plans for Germany's occupation and control and maintaining order and establishing popular Governments in liberated countries were signed yesterday by President Roosevelt, Marshal Stalin and Prime Minister Churchill near Yalta in the Crimea, the White House announced today.

The conference, held in the summer palace of former Czar Nicholas II on the Black Sea shore, also called for a United Nations security conference in San Francisco on April 25.

The parleys, hitherto shrouded in secrecy except for a brief outline of the agenda issued Feb. 7, were held day and night from Feb. 4 until the final signatures were affixed. The announcement did not refer to President Roosevelt's future movements except that he had left the Crimea.

Main Points of Accord

Major decisions of the conference include:

(1) Plans for new blows at the heart of Germany from the east, west, north and south.
(2) Agreement for occupation by the three Allies, each of a separate zone, as Germany is invaded, and an invitation to France to take over a zone and participate as a fourth member of the Control Commission.
(3) Reparations in kind to be paid by Germany for damages, to be set by an Allied commission. The reparations commission, which will establish the type and amount of payments by Germany, will have its headquarters in Moscow. [Secretary of State Stettinius and Ambassador Harriman arrived in Moscow Monday.]
(4) Settlement of questions left undecided at the conference at Dumbarton Oaks and decision to call a United Nations conference at San Francisco April 25 to prepare the charter for a general international organization to maintain peace and security.
(5) Specific agreements to widen the scope of the present Governments in Poland and Yugoslavia

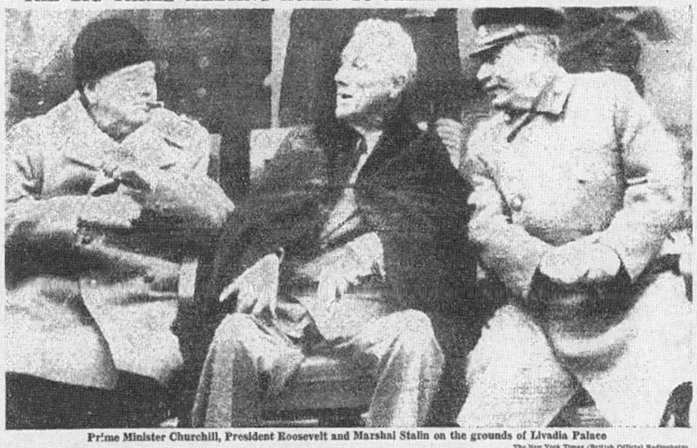

▲ Front page of *The New York Times,* February 13, 1945. (© 2007 by The New York Times Co. Reprinted with permission)

Lesson 2 Newspaper Article
Document E

Translation of Stalin's Message to the Nation
Pravda Newspaper, May 10, 1945

Comrades! Compatriots!

The great day of victory over Germany has come. Fascist Germany, brought to its knees by Red Army and Allied forces, has recognized its defeat and announced unconditional capitulation.

On May 7, the preliminary protocol of capitulation was signed in the city of Rheims. On May 8th, the representatives of Germany, in the presence of the Supreme Command of Allied forces and the High Command of Soviet Forces, signed in Berlin the final act of capitulation, which came in force on midnight May 8th.

Knowing the lupine habits of German authorities, which regard agreements as a piece of paper, we have no basis to trust their words. But from this morning on, the German troops, in fulfilling the capitulation act, started in massive scale to give up their weapons and to surrender to our troops. This is not just a piece of paper. This is the real capitulation of the armed forces of Germany. However, one group of German troops in the region of Czechoslovakia is still refusing to capitulate. But I hope that Red Army will soon successfully bring them into reality.

Now, we can rightfully announce, that the historic day of the final defeat of Germany has come. The day of the great victory of our Nation over German Imperialism.

The great sacrifice, which we had to bear in the name of freedom and the independence of our Motherland, the unaccountable hardships and losses which our Nation has suffered during the war, the tense work both at the front and in the rear which we give to the altar of victory—did not come in vain, and were crowned with complete victory over the enemy. The ancient struggle of the Slavic nations for their existence and their independence has ended with victory over the German invaders and German tyranny.

Lesson 2 Newspaper Article
Document E, continued

From now on, over Europe will fly the great flag of freedom for the nations, and peace between the nations.

Three years ago, Hitler announced to all the world that among his goals was the disintegration of the Soviet Union and tearing from it the Caucasus, Ukraine, Byelorussia, the Baltic States and other regions. He said openly: "We will destroy Russia, and she will never be able to rise again."

That was three years ago. But the crazy ideas of Hitler had no chance to become reality. The progress of the War had destroyed them completely. In fact the reality is quite opposite than the Hitlerist's mad dreams. Germany is smashed. German troops declared capitulation. The Soviet Union is celebrating victory, despite the fact that it is unwilling neither to divide nor destroy Germany.

Comrades! The Great Patriotic War has ended with our complete victory. The time of war in Europe has come to the end. The time of peaceful development has begun.

My dear compatriots, I wish you all the best with victory!

GLORY TO OUR HEROIC RED ARMY, WHO DEFENDED THE INDEPENDENCE OF OUR MOTHERLAND AND DEFEATED THE ENEMY!

GLORY TO OUR GREAT NATION, THE NATION-TRIUMPHANT!

ETERNAL GLORY TO THE HEROES WHO DIED DURING THE WAR AND GAVE THEIR LIVES FOR FREEDOM AND THE HAPPINESS OF OUR NATION!

Lesson 2 Excerpt of Document
Document F

Protocol of Proceedings of Crimea Conference, February 1945

The Crimea Conference of the heads of the Governments of the United States of America, the United Kingdom, and the Union of Soviet Socialist Republics, which took place from February 4 to 11, came to the following conclusions:

WORLD ORGANIZATION

It was decided:

1. That a United Nations conference on the proposed world organization should be summoned for Wednesday, 25 April 1945, and should be held in the United States of America.

2. The nations to be invited to this conference should be:

(a) the United Nations as they existed on 8 Feb. 1945; and

(b) Such of the Associated Nations as have declared war on the common enemy by 1 March 1945. (For this purpose, by the term "Associated Nations" was meant the eight Associated Nations and Turkey.) When the conference on world organization is held, the delegates of the United Kingdom and United States of America will support a proposal to admit to original membership two Soviet Socialist Republics, i.e., the Ukraine and White Russia.

Lesson 2 Excerpt of Document
Document F, continued

3. That the United States Government, on behalf of the three powers, should consult the Government of China and the French Provisional Government in regard to decisions taken at the present conference concerning the proposed world organization.

4. That the text of the invitation to be issued to all the nations which would take part in the United Nations conference should be as follows:

"The Government of the United States of America, on behalf of itself and of the Governments of the United Kingdom, the Union of Soviet Socialist Republics and the Republic of China and of the Provisional Government of the French Republic invite the Government of ———— to send representatives to a conference to be held on 25 April 1945, or soon thereafter, at San Francisco, in the United States of America, to prepare a charter for a general international organization for the maintenance of international peace and security.

"The above-named Governments suggest that the conference consider as affording a basis for such a Charter the proposals for the establishment of a general international organization which were made public last October as a result of the Dumbarton Oaks conference and which have now been supplemented by the following provisions for Section C of Chapter VI . . .

SOURCES Roosevelt at the Yalta Conference

Lesson 2 Excerpt of Document
Document G

Protocol of Proceedings of Crimea Conference, February 1945

DECLARATION OF LIBERATED EUROPE

The following declaration has been approved:

The Premier of the Union of Soviet Socialist Republics, the Prime Minister of the United Kingdom and the President of the United States of America have consulted with each other in the common interests of the people of their countries and those of liberated Europe. They jointly declare their mutual agreement to concert during the temporary period of instability in liberated Europe the policies of their three Governments in assisting the peoples liberated from the domination of Nazi Germany and the peoples of the former Axis satellite states of Europe to solve by democratic means their pressing political and economic problems.

The establishment of order in Europe and the rebuilding of national economic life must be achieved by processes which will enable the liberated peoples to destroy the last vestiges of nazism and fascism and to create democratic institutions of their own choice. This is a principle of the Atlantic Charter—the right of all people to choose the form of government under which they will live—the restoration of sovereign rights and self-government to those peoples who have been forcibly deprived of them by the aggressor nations.

To foster the conditions in which the liberated people may exercise these rights, the three governments will jointly assist the people in any European liberated state or former Axis state in Europe where, in their judgment conditions require,

SOURCES Roosevelt at the Yalta Conference

Lesson 2 Excerpt of Document
Document G, continued

(a) to establish conditions of internal peace; (b) to carry out emergency relief measures for the relief of distressed peoples; (c) to form interim governmental authorities broadly representative of all democratic elements in the population and pledged to the earliest possible establishment through free elections of Governments responsive to the will of the people; and (d) to facilitate where necessary the holding of such elections.

The three Governments will consult the other United Nations and provisional authorities or other Governments in Europe when matters of direct interest to them are under consideration.

When, in the opinion of the three Governments, conditions in any European liberated state or former Axis satellite in Europe make such action necessary, they will immediately consult together on the measure necessary to discharge the joint responsibilities set forth in this declaration.

By this declaration we reaffirm our faith in the principles of the Atlantic Charter, our pledge in the Declaration by the United Nations and our determination to build in cooperation with other peace-loving nations world order, under law, dedicated to peace, security, freedom and general well-being of all mankind.

In issuing this declaration, the three powers express the hope that the Provisional Government of the French Republic may be associated with them in the procedure suggested.

SOURCES Roosevelt at the Yalta Conference

Lesson 2 Excerpt of Document
Document H

Protocol of Proceedings of Crimea Conference, February 1945

POLAND

The following declaration on Poland was agreed by the conference:

A new situation has been created in Poland as a result of her complete liberation by the Red Army. This calls for the establishment of a Polish Provisional Government which can be more broadly based than was possible before the recent liberation of the western part of Poland. The Provisional Government which is now functioning in Poland should therefore be reorganized on a broader democratic basis with the inclusion of democratic leaders from Poland itself and from Poles abroad. This new Government should then be called the Polish Provisional Government of National Unity.

M. Molotov, Mr. Harriman and Sir A. Clark Kerr are authorized as a commission to consult in the first instance in Moscow with members of the present Provisional Government and with other Polish democratic leaders from within Poland and from abroad, with a view to the reorganization of the present Government along the above lines. This Polish Provisional Government of National Unity shall be pledged to the holding of free and unfettered elections as soon as possible on the basis of universal suffrage and secret ballot. In these elections all democratic and anti-Nazi parties shall have the right to take part and to put forward candidates.

SOURCES Roosevelt at the Yalta Conference

Lesson 2 Excerpt of Document
Document H, continued

When a Polish Provisional Government of National Unity has been properly formed in conformity with the above, the Government of the U.S.S.R., which now maintains diplomatic relations with the present Provisional Government of Poland, and the Government of the United Kingdom and the Government of the United States of America will establish diplomatic relations with the new Polish Provisional Government of National Unity, and will exchange Ambassadors by whose reports the respective Governments will be kept informed about the situation in Poland.

The three heads of Government consider that the eastern frontier of Poland should follow the Curzon Line with digressions from it in some regions of five to eight kilometers in favor of Poland. They recognize that Poland must receive substantial accessions in territory in the north and west. They feel that the opinion of the new Polish Provisional Government of National Unity should be sought in due course of the extent of these accessions and that the final delimitation of the western frontier of Poland should thereafter await the peace conference.

SOURCES Roosevelt at the Yalta Conference

Lesson 2 Excerpt of Document
Document I

Protocol of Proceedings of Crimea Conference, February 1945

AGREEMENT REGARDING JAPAN

The leaders of the three great powers—the Soviet Union, the United States of America and Great Britain—have agreed that in two or three months after Germany has surrendered and the war in Europe is terminated, the Soviet Union shall enter into war against Japan on the side of the Allies on condition that:

1. The status quo in Outer Mongolia (the Mongolian People's Republic) shall be preserved.

2. The former rights of Russia violated by the treacherous attack of Japan in 1904 shall be restored, viz.: (a) The southern part of Sakhalin as well as the islands adjacent to it shall be returned to the Soviet Union; (b) The commercial port of Dairen shall be internationalized, the pre-eminent interests of the Soviet Union in this port being safeguarded, and the lease of Port Arthur as a naval base of the U.S.S.R. restored; (c) The Chinese-Eastern Railroad and the South Manchurian Railroad, which provide an outlet to Dairen, shall be jointly operated by the establishment of a joint Soviet-Chinese company, it being understood that the pre-eminent interests of the Soviet Union shall be safeguarded and that China shall retain sovereignty in Manchuria;

3. The Kurile Islands shall be handed over to the Soviet Union.

It is understood that the agreement concerning Outer Mongolia and the ports and railroads referred to above will require concurrence of Generalissimo Chiang Kai-shek. The President will take measures in order to maintain this concurrence on advice from Marshal Stalin.

The heads of the three great powers have agreed that these claims of the Soviet Union shall be unquestionably fulfilled after Japan has been defeated.

For its part, the Soviet Union expresses it readiness to conclude with the National Government of China a pact of friendship and alliance between the U.S.S.R. and China in order to render assistance to China with its armed forces for the purpose of liberating China from the Japanese yoke.

(signed) Joseph Stalin, Franklin D. Roosevelt, Winston S. Churchill

February 11, 1945

BACKGROUND MATERIAL

Roosevelt at the Yalta Conference

Biographies and Organizations

James Byrnes Born in Charleston, South Carolina, on May 2, 1879, James Byrnes studied law and was admitted to the bar in 1903. His budgetary expertise was highly prized during the Great Depression and World War II. After serving in the U.S. House of Representatives, Byrnes was elected to the Senate in 1930 and re-elected in 1936. He supported President Roosevelt in foreign policy matters and helped secure the repeal of the Neutrality Act of 1935 and passage of the Lend-Lease Act of 1941. Byrnes was appointed to the Supreme Court in 1941 as an associate justice. He became the director of economic stabilization in 1942 and the director of the Office of War Mobilization in 1943. In 1945, President Truman named Byrnes secretary of state. His experiences in dealing with the Soviets convinced him that the United States needed to negotiate from strength and oppose communist expansion. He resigned in 1947 and was governor of South Carolina from 1951 to 1955. Byrnes died on April 9, 1972.

Winston Churchill Winston Churchill was born at Blenheim Palace, Woodstock, Oxfordshire, on November 30, 1874. In a versatile career that spanned four decades, he served Great Britain as a war correspondent, soldier, politician, member of the British Parliament, first lord of the Admiralty, and prime minister. A prolific writer and an eloquent orator as well, he inspired Britons with his writings and speeches during the dark days of World War II. A man of action as well as a man of words, he was an inspiring and decisive military and political leader during both world wars.

After Churchill became prime minister in May 1940, he led Britain through what many believed was the country's darkest hour. Churchill rallied the British people to what he called the ultimate fight for survival and braced the country for the German onslaught with determination. After the United States entered the war in December 1941, Churchill and Roosevelt quickly allied their efforts to form a powerful coalition, along with the Soviet Union, against the Axis powers. With an Allied victory in sight by 1944, Churchill turned his attention increasingly to the shape of the postwar world. Through a series of conferences, Churchill, Roosevelt, and Stalin hammered out tentative agreements for dealing with a defeated Germany and restoring order to the world. Earlier than his colleagues, Churchill foresaw the great struggle between communism and democracy that emerged as the Cold War. Voted out of office in July 1945, Churchill re-

▲ Winston Churchill
(Library of Congress)

BACKGROUND MATERIAL Roosevelt at the Yalta Conference

mained an international hero and proved himself an astute observer of worldwide affairs. In a 1946 speech, he warned of the developing East-West rift, stating that an "iron curtain" was dividing Europe, behind which tyranny reigned. Churchill retired from politics in 1955 and died in London on January 24, 1965.

Harry Hopkins Harry Hopkins was born on August 17, 1890, in Sioux City, Iowa, and graduated from Grinnell College in 1912. He was the principal architect of New Deal relief programs during the Great Depression. Hopkins's integrity and commitment to social work were widely admired, but his blunt and abrupt manner often alienated colleagues. In 1940, Hopkins resigned as secretary of commerce, but then served as a major foreign policy advisor to President Franklin Roosevelt. In 1941, he took on the administration of the lend-lease program, and it was largely on his recommendation that lend-lease aid was extended to the Soviet Union. Throughout World War II, Hopkins traveled around the world and met with political and military leaders on the president's behalf. Upon the death of Roosevelt in April 1945, Hopkins helped to ensure the smooth transition of the presidency to Harry Truman. He died on January 29, 1946.

Franklin D. Roosevelt Born on January 30, 1882, in Hyde Park, New York, Franklin Roosevelt attended Harvard University and Columbia University Law School. In 1921, he was stricken with polio and almost completely paralyzed. Elected president in 1932 and reelected three more times before he died near the end of World War II, Roosevelt was the only U.S. president ever to serve more than two terms. During the twelve years of his presidency, Roosevelt aroused both intense loyalty and opposition. Roosevelt's impact on the United States through his New Deal legislation during the Great Depression was huge and lasting. He died on April 12, 1945.

▲ Franklin D. Roosevelt
(Library of Congress)

Roosevelt hoped to keep the United States out of war, but as World War II began in 1939, he worked to bring about the repeal of the Neutrality Act of 1935 so that he could provide aid to Great Britain. Following his reelection in 1940, Roosevelt obtained congressional approval to provide lend-lease aid to Great Britain and the Soviet Union. After the Japanese attack at Pearl Harbor brought the United States into the war, Roosevelt behaved in characteristically pragmatic fashion; his goal was to win the war with as few American casualties as possible. To do this,

Biographies and Organizations, continued

he needed to keep the wartime alliance of Great Britain, the Soviet Union, and the United States together until after Germany and Japan were defeated, and he did. At the Allied summit at Yalta in 1945, he was unable to secure a Poland free of Soviet domination, but he did manage to obtain a Soviet promise to join the war against Japan and to participate in the United Nations. Critics attack his refusal to challenge Soviet domination of Eastern Europe, but supporters point out that it was merely an acceptance of political reality—Soviet troops occupied the region.

Joseph Stalin Born on December 21, 1879, in Gori, Georgia, Stalin grew up in poverty and uncertainty but did receive a good education. He was exposed to Marxism while attending seminary and was deeply involved in the Marxist revolutionary movement in Georgia by 1900. An important member of the Bolshevik Party during the Russian Revolution of 1917, Stalin rose to become the successor to Vladimir Lenin as the leader of the Soviet Union. Stalin shaped the early Soviet Union without regard for the consequences of his actions among the Soviet population and achieved prodigious growth and a police state of unrivaled proportions. He also led his country to victory in World War II as Russian soldiers and civilians absorbed the vast majority of casualties suffered by the Allied forces. Finally, he was one of the primary architects of the postwar world and its bipolar division between East and West. He died on March 5, 1953.

The Soviet Union advanced far into Central Europe during the final months of World War II, and by the spring of 1945, the Germans were beaten. Through a series of conferences with Allied leaders both during and immediately after the war, Stalin secured for the Soviet Union all territory in Eastern Europe occupied by the Red Army at the time of the German surrender. Stalin saw those lands not only as territory that could be exploited for the benefit of the Soviet Union, but also as a buffer zone between the Soviet Union and future attacks from the West. By the late 1940s, the boundary between the Soviet sphere and the nations of Western Europe had been christened the "iron curtain" by Winston Churchill, and the Cold War was setting in.

▲ Joseph Stalin
(Library of Congress)

BACKGROUND MATERIAL Roosevelt at the Yalta Conference

Edward R. Stettinius, Jr. A businessman and diplomat, Edward Stettinius was secretary of state during the last years of World War II and served as the first U.S. ambassador to the United Nations. Born on October 22, 1900, in Chicago, he attended the University of Virginia. Stettinius accepted an appointment to the War Resources Board in 1939. After a year on the Council of National Defense and two years as administrator of the lend-lease program, he became under secretary of state in 1943. Appointed secretary of state in 1944, Stettinius became one of President Franklin D. Roosevelt's most trusted advisors at the important Yalta Conference in 1945. Stettinius helped found the United Nations as leader of the U.S. delegation to the UN charter conference at San Francisco in April 1945. He became the first U.S. delegate to the UN in June 1945. Stettinius died on October 31, 1949.

Henry L. Stimson Henry Stimson was born on September 21, 1867, in New York City. He graduated from Yale University in 1888 and from Harvard Law School in 1890. After serving as secretary of war from 1911 to 1913, Stimson fought during World War I. In 1929, he was appointed secretary of state. After the Japanese invasion of Manchuria in 1931, he announced the Stimson Doctrine declaring the U.S. refusal to recognize the annexation of territory through aggression. Roosevelt appointed Stimson secretary of war in 1940, and he energetically oversaw the creation of the mammoth American military-industrial complex. In 1945, as the chief presidential advisor on atomic policy, Stimson recommended the dropping of atomic bombs on Japanese cities. He later defended his controversial recommendation as necessary to avoid the sacrifice of American soldiers in a costly invasion. Stimson retired at the end of World War II and died on October 20, 1950.

▲ Henry L. Stimson
(Library of Congress)

United Nations (UN) Established in the aftermath of World War II in an attempt to stabilize international relations and create a firm foundation for peace, the United Nations has served as a sort of watchdog to the world for more than fifty years. The UN's original definition as an association of independent and sovereign states established "to maintain international peace and security" and to promote international cooperation for the creation of positive political, economic, and social conditions has

BACKGROUND MATERIAL Roosevelt at the Yalta Conference

Biographies and Organizations, continued

placed the organization in the center of various tragedies, scandals, and triumphs. With headquarters in New York City, the UN continues to take a firm hand in world events.

President Franklin Roosevelt first used the term "United Nations" in the Declaration by United Nations written during World War II, in which representatives of twenty-six nations pledged that their governments would continue fighting as allies against the Axis powers. After meetings between representatives of major world powers in August–October 1944, the UN charter was drafted in San Francisco from April 25 to June 26, 1945, at the United Nations Conference on International Organization by representatives of fifty countries. The charter was ratified by the necessary number of states on October 24, 1945, and the UN officially came into being.

BACKGROUND MATERIAL Roosevelt at the Yalta Conference

Key Events

Cairo Conferences The Cairo Conferences were held by British prime minister Winston Churchill and U.S. president Franklin D. Roosevelt during World War II in Cairo, Egypt. The first conference took place during November 22–26, 1943. Churchill and Roosevelt discussed plans for the D-Day invasion of Normandy. The two leaders also met with Chinese Nationalist leader Chiang Kai-shek to discuss the war against Japan. They resolved to liberate the Pacific islands Japan had seized, and they agreed to return lost territory to China and to establish an independent Korea after the war. The Allies were not able to decide on specific military strategies. The second conference was held after the Tehran Conference—the first meeting between all the major Allied leaders—on December 2–7, 1943. Churchill and Roosevelt unsuccessfully lobbied Turkey to join the Allied war effort. Roosevelt also informed Churchill of the decision to have U.S. general Dwight D. Eisenhower lead the D-Day invasion.

Potsdam Conference From July 17 to August 2, 1945, Harry Truman, Winston Churchill (replaced by the new prime minister Clement Attlee on July 28), and Joseph Stalin met in Potsdam, Germany, in the final wartime conference between the Allies. Germany had surrendered on May 8, but Japan continued to fight. They issued Japan an ultimatum on July 26 to surrender unconditionally or be destroyed. The rest of the conference was devoted to the arrangement of postwar Europe. Soviet control of Eastern Europe was tacitly recognized by the Western powers and provisions were made for dividing Berlin into four quadrants, each to be ruled by one of the Allies (including France). A number of agreements were reached over the reestablishment of governments and economies in the defeated countries. Truman received word of the successful testing of the atomic bomb and informed Churchill, casually mentioning it to Stalin without providing any details. Differences between the United States and the Soviet Union began to emerge clearly at this conference and many consider it the start of the Cold War.

Tehran Conference From November 28 to December 1, 1943, President Franklin D. Roosevelt, Premier Joseph Stalin, and Prime Minister Winston Churchill held their first meeting in Tehran, Iran, during World War II. The progress of the war dominated the content of the meeting. Preliminary discussions

Key Events, continued

included an attempt to convince Turkey to join the war and further Allied operations. Recently captured by the Nazis, Finland also became an issue. Eastern Europe was a contentious issue; damaged more than other nations by the war, the Soviet Union looked to gain greater control of territory there to compensate for German aggression. The postwar boundaries of Poland and Germany thus became issues of serious debate. Although the meeting accomplished little, it set the stage for later and more productive meetings regarding postwar Europe. It also symbolized the future nature of the Allies' relationship: military alignment rather than genuine international cooperation.

World War II World War II was the largest and most destructive conflict fought in human history. In Asia, hostilities began with the Japanese invasion of Manchuria in 1931. In Europe, the war began in September 1939 when Germany invaded Poland. The United States joined the war after Japan launched a surprise air attack on the U.S. naval base at Pearl Harbor, Hawaii, on December 7, 1941.

In the opening months of U.S. involvement in the war, the Japanese quickly overran American forces in much of the Pacific theater. Adopting the strategy of "island hopping," American forces took control of the many isolated Japanese outposts in the Pacific and gradually closed in on mainland Japan. After atomic bombs were dropped on the Japanese cities of Hiroshima and Nagasaki at President Truman's order, Japan unconditionally surrendered on September 2, 1945.

In Europe, the Nazis had conquered much of the continent and huge stretches of the Soviet Union by the end of 1941. By January 1943, the Battle of Stalingrad had marked a turning point on the eastern front. Allied efforts on the western front culminated on June 6, 1944, when Allied forces successfully landed on the coast of France in the D-Day invasion. In December

BACKGROUND MATERIAL Roosevelt at the Yalta Conference

1944, the Germans mounted one final desperate and unsuccessful offensive during the Battle of the Bulge. The Soviets captured Berlin by the end of April 1945, and Germany surrendered unconditionally on May 8.

About fifty million people died during the war and the conflict consumed at least $2 trillion of the world's wealth. Europe was in ruins. The use of atomic weapons forever altered calculations about international relations and military power. The United States and the Soviet Union emerged as the two dominant superpowers and now faced each other in an increasingly hostile Cold War that pitted capitalism and communism against each other.

Yalta Conference The Allies gathered at the Crimean Peninsula city of Yalta on February 4–11, 1945, to decide the fate of post–World War II Germany and resolve other issues. The meeting included Soviet leader Joseph Stalin, British prime minister Winston Churchill, and U.S. president Franklin D. Roosevelt. The three leaders planned to split Germany into four occupation zones with France as the fourth occupying power. The meeting also called for Germany to pay the Soviet Union war reparations. The Soviet Union was given great influence over most of Eastern Europe, while the United States seized the opportunity to promote the establishment of a world organization to maintain the postwar peace. Another meeting was scheduled for April 1945 at which the UN would be established. In exchange for territory in the Far East, Stalin also promised that he would declare war on Japan within ninety days of Germany's surrender.

BACKGROUND MATERIAL Roosevelt at the Yalta Conference

Excerpts from Declarations, Charters, and Treaties

Yalta Conference (1945)
I. WORLD ORGANIZATION

1. That a United Nations conference on the proposed world organization should be summoned for Wednesday, 25 April 1945, and should be held in the United States of America.

II. DECLARATION OF LIBERATED EUROPE

The establishment of order in Europe and the rebuilding of national economic life must be achieved by processes which will enable the liberated peoples to destroy the last vestiges of nazism and fascism and to create democratic institutions of their own choice.

IV. ZONE OF OCCUPATION FOR THE FRENCH AND CONTROL COUNCIL FOR GERMANY

It was agreed that a zone in Germany, to be occupied by the French forces, should be allocated to France. This zone would be formed out of the British and American zones and its extent would be settled by the British and Americans in consultation with the French Provisional Government.

V. REPARATION

1. Germany must pay in kind for the losses caused by her to the Allied nations in the course of the war. Reparations are to be received in the first instance by those countries which have borne the main burden of the war. . . .

AGREEMENT REGARDING JAPAN

The leaders of the three great powers . . . have agreed that in two or three months after Germany has surrendered and the war in Europe is terminated, the Soviet Union shall enter into war against Japan on the side of the Allies. . . .

United Nations: Charter (1945)
ARTICLE 1

The Purposes of the United Nations are:

1. To maintain international peace and security, and to that end: to take effective collective measures for the prevention and removal of threats to the peace, and for the suppression of acts of aggression or other breaches of the peace, and to bring about by peaceful means, and in conformity with the principles of justice

and international law, adjustment or settlement of international disputes or situations which might lead to a breach of the peace;

3. To achieve international cooperation in solving international problems of an economic, social, cultural, or humanitarian character, and in promoting and encouraging respect for human rights and for fundamental freedoms for all without distinction as to race, sex, language, or religion; and

ARTICLE 2

4. All Members shall refrain in their international relations from the threat or use of force against the territorial integrity or political independence of any state, or in any other manner inconsistent with the Purposes of the United Nations.

United Nations: Universal Declaration of Human Rights (1948)

ARTICLE 1

All human beings are born free and equal in dignity and rights. They are endowed with reason and conscience and should act towards one another in a spirit of brotherhood.

ARTICLE 2

Everyone is entitled to all the rights and freedoms set forth in this Declaration, without distinction of any kind, such as race, colour, sex, language, religion, political or other opinion, national or social origin, property, birth or other status.

Furthermore, no distinction shall be made on the basis of the political, jurisdictional or international status of the country or territory to which a person belongs, whether it be independent, trust, non-self-governing or under any other limitation of sovereignty.

ARTICLE 7

All are equal before the law and are entitled without any discrimination to equal protection of the law. All are entitled to equal protection against any discrimination in violation of this Declaration and against any incitement to such discrimination.

Excerpts from Declarations, Charters, and Treaties, continued

Atlantic Charter (1941)
The President of the United States of America and the Prime Minister, Mr. Churchill, representing His Majesty's Government in the United Kingdom, being met together, deem it right to make known certain common principles in the national policies of their respective countries on which they base their hopes for a better future for the world.

First, their countries seek no aggrandizement, territorial or other;

Second, they desire to see no territorial changes that do not accord with the freely expressed wishes of the peoples concerned;

Third, they respect the right of all peoples to choose the form of government under which they will live; and they wish to see sovereign rights and self-government restored to those who have been forcibly deprived of them; . . .

Sixth, after the final destruction of the Nazi tyranny, they hope to see established a peace which will afford to all nations the means of dwelling in safety within their own boundaries, and which will afford assurance that all the men in all lands may live out their lives in freedom from fear and want; . . .

Eighth, they believe that all of the nations of the world, for realistic as well as spiritual reasons must come to the abandonment of the use of force.

Declaration on Liberated Europe (1945)
Declaration issued by leaders of the United States, Great Britain, and the Soviet Union—the "Big Three"—during the February 1945 Yalta Conference. It affirmed the right of all peoples "to choose the government under which they will live" and called for the "restoration of sovereign rights and self-government" to peoples who had been occupied by the "aggressor nations." The Big Three pledged that in the liberated nations, they would work to restore internal peace, relieve distress, form govern-

BACKGROUND MATERIAL Roosevelt at the Yalta Conference

ments that were "broadly representative of all democratic elements in the population," and ensure that there would be "free elections" as soon as possible.

No institutional arrangement was established to enforce the ideas embodied in the declaration. As it transpired, the Soviets chose to regard "democratic elements" as meaning all communist and pro-communist factions and "free elections" as excluding all those they regarded to be fascists. The result was Soviet control over much of eastern and central Europe—at first indirect and, with the development of the Cold War, direct.

ADDITIONAL RESOURCES

- Integration into National History Day
- Using ABC-CLIO Websites for Researching the Presidency
- Additional Presidency Topic Ideas

ADDITIONAL RESOURCES

Integration into National History Day

The Office of the President is confronted with conflict and compromise daily. Although a president is challenged to resolve domestic and international conflicts, it is the international conflicts that often are the "defining moments" for American presidents. How a president reacts to conflicts or settles conflicts through a compromise becomes fascinating political research for National History Day students.

National History Day (NHD) is an educational program engaging students in grades 6–12 in historical research. After selecting a topic related to the NHD annual theme, students conduct research into primary and secondary sources. They enter projects in competitions using one of four different presentation formats: paper, performance, exhibit, or documentary.

Research projects on *The Presidency* could encourage students to present a paper on the compromises and impact of the Treaty of Versailles or the conflict caused by the compromises of Yalta. Another student might choose to focus on domestic issues and create a documentary examining the Compromise of 1877 or the conflicts and compromises of the period of Reconstruction. An exhibit constructed of the internal and external conflict of antebellum politics and the great personal sacrifices of Abraham Lincoln may well illuminate the power of the decision-making process of an American president. A historical performance of John F. Kennedy and Fidel Castro focused on the power of conflict to ignite or avoid a nuclear war will lead to a greater understanding of the power of compromise.

National History Day invites students to determine the historical significance of their chosen topic. Projects related to *The Presidency* can be approached using different research processes:

- Using primary and secondary documents to place the topic in historical perspectives

- Building a timeline of events leading to the conflict to illustrate the significance of the topic

- Presenting an analysis of the conflict through the introduction of the historical context and people involved to deepen historical understanding

ADDITIONAL RESOURCES

Regardless of the topic or approach, students should ask questions of their research and the meaning of their topic in history.

- Who were the people involved?
- What were their motivations?
- Why did the incident occur at this time in history?
- What was gained and what price was paid?
- What was the legacy of the decision to escalate the conflict or reach a compromise?
- What if the opposing choice had been made? How would that have impacted our world of today?

Complete guidelines and more information can be accessed at www.nhd.org

ADDITIONAL RESOURCES

Using ABC-CLIO Websites for Researching the Presidency

The ABC-CLIO Schools Social Studies subscription websites combine reference material, curriculum, current events, and primary sources in a single resource to help make historical research straightforward, accessible, and exciting for students. They provide students with the tools they need to investigate and assess the important questions associated with the topic of the presidency.

Questions to consider:

- How important is the use of compromise and diplomacy in presidential foreign policy? What developments have affected the importance of diplomacy throughout U.S. history?

- Why have Congress and the president tended to clash over war powers throughout U.S. history? How did that conflict play out in the twentieth century?

- Why did the United States adopt a policy of isolationism in foreign affairs for much of its history? What factors caused a shift to interventionism in the twentieth century?

- What role does public opinion play in influencing foreign policy? How and why has the influence of public opinion changed over time?

With these websites, students can find entries related to the topic of the presidency that link to related reference and primary source material, providing historical context that will help students develop their skills of source evaluation and historical analysis. Teachers can construct customized research lists of reference entries, images, maps, and documents, enabling students to compare, contrast, and analyze a variety of related resources.

ABC-CLIO'S SOCIAL STUDIES SUBSCRIPTION WEBSITES

- Provide students access to deeper and broader content than other social studies resources, allowing them to synthesize what they learn from reference material and primary sources
- Combine reference, curriculum, and descriptions of current events, which are updated daily
- Are correlated to curriculum standards, key assessments, and major textbooks
- Meet the needs of students for different grade levels and assignments
- Provide access from school and home for students and faculty

Additional Presidency Topic Ideas

1. George Washington and the Birth of Isolationism
2. John Adams and the XYZ Affair
3. Conflict with Great Britain: Jefferson, Madison, and the War of 1812
4. Evaluating the Monroe Doctrine
5. The Role of Popular Ideology: Manifest Destiny and War
6. Preventing Foreign Intervention: Lincoln and the American Civil War
7. Military Interventions in Latin America
8. Race and Imperialism: The Spanish-American War
9. Theodore Roosevelt and "Big Stick" Diplomacy
10. Truman and the Berlin Airlift
11. Truman and the United Nations: The Korean War
12. Cold War Foreign Policy: NSC 68 and the "Domino Theory"
13. The Cold War Heats Up: Cuban Missile Crisis
14. Cold War Negotiations: Détente in the 1970s
15. Jimmy Carter and the Iran Hostage Crisis
16. Closed-Door Diplomacy: Iran-Contra Scandal
17. The Growth of Neoconservatism: Jeane Kirkpatrick and the Reagan Era
18. Presidential War Powers: Congressional Acts and Resolutions in the Twentieth Century
19. Isolationism vs. Interventionism
20. Presidential Prerogative: America's Undeclared Wars